Saga / Circus

Saga / Circus

Lyn Hejinian

OMNIDAWN PUBLISHING
RICHMOND, CALIFORNIA
2008

Book cover art and design: Ree Katrak
Interior Art: Emilie Clark
Book interior design by Ken Keegan.

Offset printed in the United States on archival, acid-free recycled paper
by Thomson-Shore, Inc., Dexter, Michigan

Omnidawn Publishing is committed to preserving ancient forests and natural resources. We elected to print this title on 30% postconsumer recycled paper, processed chlorine-free. As a result, for this printing, we have saved:

3 Trees (40' tall and 6-8" diameter)
1,127 Gallons of Wastewater
2 million BTUs of Total Energy
125 Pounds of Solid Waste
245 Pounds of Greenhouse Gases

Omnidawn Publishing made this paper choice because our printer, Thomson-Shore, Inc., is a member of Green Press Initiative, a nonprofit program dedicated to supporting authors, publishers, and suppliers in their efforts to reduce their use of fiber obtained from endangered forests.

For more information, visit www.greenpressinitiative.org

Environmental impact estimates were made using the Environmental Defense Paper Calculator. For more information visit: www.edf.org/papercalculator

Library of Congress Catalog-in-Publication Data

Hejinian, Lyn.
Saga/circus / Lyn Hejinian.
p. cm.
ISBN 978-1-890650-34-6 (pbk. : alk. paper)
I. Title.
PS3558.E4735S24 2008
811'.54--dc22

2008029442

Published by Omnidawn Publishing, Richmond, California
www.omnidawn.com (510) 237-5472 (800) 792-4957
10 9 8 7 6 5 4 3 2 1

ISBN: 978-1-890650-34-6

Previous Books By Lyn Hejinian

Poetry

Lola (belladonna, 2005)
My Life in the Nineties (Shark Books, 2003)
The Fatalist (Omnidawn, 2003)
On Laughter: A Melodrama
(written with Jack Collom; Baksun Books, 2003)
Slowly (Tuumba Press, 2002)
A Border Comedy (Granary Books, 2001)
The Beginner (Spectacular Books, 2000; Tuumba Press, 2002)
Happily (Post-Apollo Press, 2000)
Chartings (written with Ray Di Palma; Chax Press, 2000)
Sunflower (written with Jack Collom; The Figures, 2000)
Sight (written with Leslie Scalapino; Edge Books, 1999)
Wicker (written with Jack Collom; Rodent Press, 1996)
The Little Book of A Thousand Eyes
(Smoke-Proof Press, 1996)
Guide, Grammar, Watch, and The Thirty Nights
(Australia: Folio, 1996)
The Cold of Poetry (Sun & Moon Press, 1994)
The Cell (Sun & Moon Press, 1992)
The Hunt (Spain: Zasterle Press, 1991)
Oxota: A Short Russian Novel (The Figures, 1991)
Individuals (written with Kit Robinson; Chax Press, 1988)
The Guard (Tuumba Press, 1984)
Redo (Salt-Works Press, 1984)
My Life (Burning Deck, 1980; expanded version Sun & Moon, 1987)
Gesualdo (Tuumba Press, 1978)
Writing is an Aid to Memory
(The Figures, 1978; reprinted by Sun & Moon, 1996)
A Mask of Motion (Burning Deck, 1977)
A Thought is the Bride of What Thinking (Tuumba Press, 1976)

Critical Prose:

The Grand Piano: An Experiment in Collective Autobiography, (written with Rae Armantrout, Steve Benson, Carla Harryman, Tom Mandel, Ted Pearson, Bob Perelman, Kit Robinson, Ron Silliman, and Barrett Watten; Mode A, 2006–2009)

The Language of Inquiry (University of California Press, 2000)

Two Stein Talks (Weaselsleeves Press, 1995)

Leningrad (written with Michael Davidson, Ron Silliman, Barrett Watten) (Mercury House, 1991)

Acknowledgements

A selection of "chapters" from "Lola" was published as a belladonna chapbook (# 70; winter 2005); my thanks to Rachel Levitsky and Erica Kaufman for the encouragement this provided.

Early versions of some sections of "The Distance" appeared originally in *Conjunctions*, *Discourse*, and the anthology *Technologies of Measure: A Celebration of Bay Area Women Writers.* I am grateful to Bradford Morrow, Jalal Toufic, and Elizabeth Treadwell Jackson for their support.

It being my habit to elaborate imaginatively on whatever I happen to be reading at any given time, it is certain that language and ideas from various texts have made their way into *Saga / Circus*, but, to the best of my knowledge, there are only a few passages that contain direct quotations.

The reference in "Lola" to "a Russian novel" on page 44 is to Leo Tolstoy's *Anna Karenina* and the two quotes are taken from the Richard Pevear-Larissa Volokhonsky translation.

The reference on page 73 to a "a poem" is to Amiri Baraka's "A Poem Some People will Have to Understand," the quoted line comes at the end of that poem.

The phrase "sultry August dusk time than death dumber," quoted in section XVIII of "The Distance," is from "Laventie" by Ivor Gurney. Written just after World War I, upon Gurney's return from the trenches, the poem speaks of "the being afraid / Before strafes, sultry August dusk time than death dumber— / And the cooler hush after the strafe, and the long night wait—" (lines 19-20).

The descriptive image in section XV of "humans … so huge they could wade across the sea" is taken from Lucretius, *De Rerum Natura,* I, ll 200-01.

The image in section XXV of "a sheep that's lain down exhausted by its very plumpness" is also from Lucretius (I, ll 258-59).

The phrase "a series of hesitations among anomalies" in section XV can be found in Georgio Agamben, *The End of the Poem*, 46

All other quotations are cited in the text.

"Lola" is dedicated to Carla Harryman

"The Distance" is dedicated to Emilie Clark

gratefully

with admiration
and
with love

Circus

Lola

The dog on its leash knows the secret of freedom.
This is promising, says Lola.
Fanfare and ridiculous light.
Chapter One.

Chapter One

Even before I existed, says Lola, I was already at work on myself, I came prepared.

Along comes Lola.

Along comes Bill in boots apparently.

It is much easier to be enthusiastic about what exists than about what doesn't.

Air and screams, too, rubble, flitting litter, shadows, and all the rest slowly in disequilibrium kept indefinitely before the senses of the payers by players yearning to share all their pleasure mercilessly, as if this were what they'd prepared for: that: to show their pleasure mercilessly.

Chapter Two

It is not evident to the payers that all possible outcomes, all possible ends are already anachronistic and always would unjustly become so.

Romo Martinez says, the price of entry is just a starting point, you need not just words but a sense of words to see why getting in with a ticket isn't the same as getting in with the lion, Sylvia Martinez says, or with her tamer, Romo Martinez says, —or with her tameness! Sylvia Martinez says—for whom the show is always already underway, or one of those fat gray pigeons, she adds, that waddle in for free.

Sylvia Martinez believes that no crime is free of history and says so and says the same can be said of love, Romo, running her hand down his arm going to see why Memo is crying.

Chapter One

Chapters admit events, chapters worlds apart, chapters in a mood, mid-air, in plumes.

Sam comes along with binoculars, cash, gloves, a bridle, and a net, he says, there's a bird—with a rat!—and there are payers.

There are didacts, a killer, one polymath, a mother, a Russian gymnast, occasional passersby and idle salespeople, a juggler, a man with a sore throat, and a sorrowful child with cold hands and a three-legged dog on a leash, and all of these are players.

The sisters Hertha!

Drew!

Nina!

Abdul Tommy Ahmed!

Trish O'Reilly!

Kurt Krakauer!

Ludmilla Kaipa!

And Sue!

Chapter One

Quindlan is obsessed, but what are the objects of his obsession, they are paltry, but what else would you expect the objects of obsession to be, that's obsession.

Nina Lee is running the palm of her hand over the heads of the weeds, Sally Dover is teaching the children a lesson.

Chapter Two

Maggie Fornetti walks by quickly in her left hand holding an iPod adjusting her headphones with her right.

Askari Nate Martin's calm strikes Maggie Fornetti as hostile.

He can imagine her going off to some weird place no one's ever heard of and coming back with an exotic wolfish sort of cat or rodent to exhibit before some startled audience forming a circle around the thing.

Askari Nate Martin is troubled, Maggie pretends not to see him hoping he will greet her, he nods indifferently and passes by unhappily.

Maggie tends to listen to pieces of music until she can no longer hear anything of them except her responses to her experiences of them which are often more of things or thoughts that occur while she's listening than of the pieces exactly, she thinks, in pieces.

When causes can't be repeated, you infer them from effects.

Chapter Three

Helen breaks three eggs into a bowl, watching them slide and settle, the glistening yolk of the first a rich, almost orange yellow, the yolk of the second delicately pale, and on the yolk of the third gleams a single red dot.

Shoot!

Long shadows soldier through the grass, across the creek, into the silent surface along the rough front of the redwood forest.

Maggie Fornetti thinks no more about me than a bear does about Freud, Marx, or Darwin, thinks Askari Nate Martin.

Tony Parker's worst thoughts cycle swiftly round his consciousness disturbing it as a speeding jeep disturbs roadside weeds.

Askari Nate Martin is one of those clowns whose job it is to stick people's noses in their own misery, Tony tells Nina, and she says in return, we cast our own selves in a ridiculous light.

Chapter One

From inside the local library, Maggie Fornetti glances out the window, a white cat goes by with the sadness of a non-sequitur.

In the index of the book in her hand Maggie Fornetti finds desire, circulation of as compared to circulation of news, unattainability of the object of, unknowability of the attained object of, and she finds armies, disappearances into, disbanding of, fielding of, formation of, servicing of, and history, private, public, shared, suppressed.

Maggie Fornetti finds interruption, as alienating, as productive, spectacle as, see history.

Through a gap on the shelf between two dark books Maggie sees a small man an aisle over silently dancing as he reads, why not, she takes down another book, Saramago's *All the Names*, she opens it at random to page 34 and reads that "We live so sunk in ourselves that we don't notice that what is actually happening to us leaves intact, at every moment, what might happen to us."

Chapter on the Side of One, Two, Three

Every child early on should be taught to apologize, says Sally Dover.

According to Sally Dover the goal of education is improvement, the goal of self-education self-improvement, and she asks Jeanie's mother Minnie Jones, How systematic are Jeanie's efforts to improve?

How systematic are yours? Minnie asks in return indignantly, don't be defensive, Sally Dover quips, are you crazy! Minnie declares, and the exchange of bad pleasantries comes to an end.

Three must wait for one to be subtracted to be two.

Children must be very patient in order to be educated.

Jeanie while being patient picks her nose.

Just down the way Helen is plucking hairs from her chin as she addresses them impatiently, you'll no longer inhabit this continent.

Helen has fine handwriting and she displays it to herself in a green and black hardcover notebook in letters addressed to herself, Dear Helen, Quindlan is afraid.

Lola cycles past a telephone pole studded with staples.

Two little girls in pigtails snarl and paw the air and are jerked back onto their chairs.

Chapter Two

We are sentimental because we have a sense of time, Quindlan says, we have a sense of time because we can only take in so much of the world, we attend and withdraw, attend and withdraw, and that withdrawing is the tick we hear, the shutter clicking—time consists of our recurrent shutting and knowing that we shut, regretting what we miss and remembering in images—rank sentimentality!

Quindlan's anxieties began early in childhood, he likes to compartmentalize.

So they say, Fred says.

Helen eats a wedge of cheese and squeals with delight.

It's when I tell you what I'm thinking or describe to you something I've seen that I feel least understood, Helen says to Sam.

Chapter Between Two and Three

Lola has a bicycle for getting around like a weaver, and she gets around a Bible-pusher and still has the wool she's gathered, a ghastly shade of blue.

Comma, bird, and what.

The bicycle is silver but its seat is red and at the end of each of the two rubber handlebar grips is a large white glittering rhinestone star, its reflective properties satisfy safety codes, Lola is unlikely to get sideswiped.

Apostrophe, beloved, and a fast watch.

Lola goes a long distance, turns several corners always to the left, negotiates an intersection, and pedals up a hill without giving much thought to it, and she's back in a flash as a player in a film, midscreen.

She comes into a forest, sunlight and shadow dappling the ground, blue jays squawk, and she rides in a battered taxi through a big city in the rain as the driver hits the horn, she's on a military ship moving through a swell in or out of harbor in the fog past a ringing bell buoy standing beside a young sailor in a watchcap.

People often do things without any consciousness of why or how, they can't retrace their path, although they might inadvertently and without noticing it go exactly the same way again past a log swept down from the forest and bobbing amid chrysanthemum heads, plastic tassels, and other flotsam on the waves.

Montgomery appears with a pie in search of a fount of money.

How will the money stay crisp in the mist.

There are many more comings and goings than this and only three chapters, and we must find their explanation elsewhere if we can, but it's unlikely that we can, the superego forbids without our knowing what's forbidden, producing ruptures or seeming to, breaking things up, but inevitably something comes along to fill the gap, monotony, a river rolling over rocks for example despite the tiger on its bank eating a dog, which will cause the passersby along with the players to thank their stars for the other-sidedness of the river or the this-sidedness of art, in art, blood isn't bloody, it just rhymes with 'flood.'

Worry with story, archer with anchor and with a bow, anchor with anger with execution and a bow with a crow cawing in a live oak tree under which lie thorny leaves, Lola bicycles by, riding through the leaves, a dog is commanded to sit, a child to apologize.

Lola pursues the logics of her interest, through the rubble and over the sill.

Chapter Supplied

What do we know about birds, asks Sally Dover, they have feathers, says Jeanie Jones with pleasure, Lola says, they fly, cooperatively, not penguins, says Memo, Graciela Parker says, they lay eggs, they nest, says Jeanie Jones, what, asks Lola, do birds know about us?

Sally Dover says nothing.

Chapter Three

Along comes Mrs. Sally Dover.

It's now after 4, now after school, Mrs. Sally Dover is wearing yellow, violet, blue, she has semblance, her memories are trapezed.

It's now after all.

It has always been for Sally Dover, thinks Sally Dover, not chapter one but chapter three.

Resentment never loses its specificity.

Resentment takes itself to itself.

Resentment continues, talking to itself, Sally Dover, she laughs at what she has, what she hears, but the laughter's a far cry from merriment, she's always hated the carousel with its turning and terrifying horses getting nowhere, hating herself, she's happiest at home aloft in her yellow pajamas.

When she complains her allusions are anything but vague, she never says "Women!" when she means Nina Lee, though when she says "Nina Lee hates me" she means that women hate her.

Mothers are always suspicious of their children's teacher, says Minnie Jones, who isn't trying to comfort Sally Dover but only to dispel her anxiety, i.e. to make her shut up.

They love you, says Sally Dover bitterly.

Sally Dover is thirty-two.

Chapter Two

I wanted there always to be someone in my life who'd be immediately and completely pleased by my successes, says Helen to Sam.

Those would be your parents, says Sam, Sam is settling.

You're quoting wisdom from the Book of Cowardice, says Helen who's been reading Oscar Wilde while waiting in the car, she has a fleck of chocolate on her lower lip.

Chapter One

Sid is a young Marine, Quindlan is a player, Mrs. Lee is climbing the stairs and in the grocery bag she holds in her arms are a starfish, a potato, a bottle of syrup, a map of Minnesota, a misspelled word, a sample of satin, and an ominous owl, a scream.

Then along comes Chapter Two for which everyone must practice constantly and with it comes Chapter 3.

Chapter 3 and Chapter Two

The apple in fall comes to rest near a man with his fortune rolled up in a ball that he caught on a dare as it bounced off a car, the door slightly ajar, a strange smell in the air.

The lovers tumble to the side of spontaneity without wondering what it's for, what it can do, and declare it "an un-in-ter-rup-ted round of pleasure!"

Along comes a juggler with a treasure hiding jars in the air made bright by the sun in the eyes of the lover, a beholder.

A small cop tumbles into view, happening onto the scene without a clue as if at fate's request to find a guy left high and dry whom he can arrest.

Symptomatically belligerently Quindlan asks, What's dubious about Fritos?

Did you know that cats that purr don't roar and cats that roar don't purr? Maggie Fornetti asks Askari Nate Martin, who thinks perhaps he's being grilled.

Helen says paranoia is archaic, Maggie says, full of old surprises.

Askari Nate Martin notes that conversations in real life rarely move directly from A (derived from elements of the theme being developed) to B (derived from completely different elements using completely different talents) but still the conversations give birth to the image in which the matter is most clearly embodied.

The juggler juggles with jugs that have been prepared, the tumbler is him or herself prepared.

The result will produce in the payers a complete image but of something bearing little relation to the bigger theme.

Chapter Between

I haven't far to go, says Mrs. Lee in motley.

Lola whose point of view we can almost see assists Mrs. Lee.

Seven packages, Mrs. Lee!

Yes, dear, but none for me, look at these, a set of Fridays, and a stunt, and a long story laid out lazily, she says, setting down a sack from which an apple rolls, a beautiful green Gravenstein.

Lola listens, lingering fleetingly balancing bicycle and packages, one of which holds music—music is the assassin of ancestors.

At my age, says Mrs. Lee, I'm like a clown occupying a senseless point at the center of a ring, and look at you! you run rings around me!

I've been to Salinas, Lola says, and before that Eureka and San Jose.

Chapter Two

Askari Nate Martin, when inspired by love, takes note with a silent nod intended to point out things that he loves to the one he loves as his love, but Maggie Fornetti when it comes to love wants more than a nod, more than shadowboxing, Take that! and that! and that! she says to herself sarcastically dismally.

A strong wind is blowing rings around them, hardly noticeable at first, shadows flit, leaves pretending to dance with themselves flirt with the shadows, but now shadows and leaves are dodging, ducking, seeking refuge behind each other, done with dancing and then with batting at each other, they would gladly drag whole trees after them to escape the wind.

I'm not sheltered in arms, Maggie Fornetti thinks to herself involuntarily, touching her hip bones through her coat pockets.

Pleasantly aware of appearing thoughtful, watching Maggie thinks of Nate investigating, going on with only what he calls Piece A and Piece B.

Askari Nate Martin is making Maggie Fornetti anxious, his maneuvers provoke anxiety (desire), in an effort to alleviate her anxiety she thinks she should throw herself into his path.

Piece C, she says to him, connects them—it comes between them, not after.

Chapter If It's True

Graciela Parker says, guys, to Jeanie Jones and Lola, I know, let's eat our snacks at the fort, it's very foggy, says Jeanie Jones, if the sky comes all the way down to the ground, then everything's blue all around, says Lola, Graciela Parker says, whatever, even if we can't see it, asks Jeanie Jones.

Lola enchants the world, she takes it to be real.

Chapters Nine to Five

9

A business succeeds by using the world as if it were a magician's prop or a crystal ball whose secret a medium is about to reveal as if it contained a fragrant drop in the shower of good will.

Overhead a hawk circles.

Fredo, says Frankie slightly tilting his head, what if we were to make dustclothes out of cashmere or shovels out of silver?

Money has no memory—it forgets what it paid for, shows no trace of where it's been or why.

Every footprint on the path is obliterated, every detail melts away, all that's left is mud, the whole of everything, producing a kind of mystical pleasure that makes me want to, you know, Fredo says to Frankie, set sail or (pulling off his watchcap and rubbing his palm over his scalp) piss with my legs spread like a girl's like a horse leaving a puddle, the steam coming up, rising, intimately smelly, Fredo, Frankie says, there is just as much rapture to be had in making a cocoon as in emerging from it.

Before it's too late, the company comes out for a bow.

8

Why is it that so many of Walmart's employees have greyhounds, asks the older of the sisters Hertha, they don't, says the younger, it must be a matter of calories, says the older, on thin dogs the veins can be found more easily, says the younger, and on shorthairs the nails are more easily seen, says the older, they're unnatural, says the younger and faster, they don't run from tyrants but for them.

The voice of the younger sister Hertha is hoarser than her sister's, the legs of the younger are fatter, the sadness of both is no deeper than the water in the bathtub out of which the knees of the older jut, like pilings against which the younger's rapidly flowing thoughts swirl.

The grotesque visions that emerge in self-loathing themselves flow, which is lucky for us, says the older sister Hertha, sending them on their way.

The older sister Hertha has a splendid memory for good memories and she can count on them to bring her round to a better way of thinking, the younger sister feels it imperative to remain vulnerable to reprimand.

7

We have to eat to live, Helen says, slapping a package of chicken thighs onto the counter beside a plastic basket of strawberries, a jar of mustard, two yams, a head of red leaf lettuce, a dozen extra large eggs, a pound of butter, an avocado, a bag of chocolate chip oatmeal cookies, two bottles of cheap wine, and a copy of *People* magazine, as she looks to her left at Sid and laughs.

Sid is buying a map and a disposable camera, an apple, a loaf of bread, and a six-pack of beer, Helen points to the camera, then flutters her hands, and says as for me I can't seem to get a good picture even with a point and shoot, Helen is just exiting a period of happiness.

Tiny Toscano has possibilities she can't exhaust.

6

The man who wants to be good just wants to be a god with nothing, says Drew to Montgomery, as one man might say to another who resembles or perhaps is the old friend with whom he used to go camping but he could just as well be a perfect stranger, hammering in one tent peg as Montgomery hammers in another.

The wind is picking up dust, some bits of string, a whiff of fart from Pépé, Helen's flatulent white dog who's lying nearby in the golden light of the late afternoon which is flickering like the distance seen through a fire in daylight.

Bill calls Helen's dog Peppy, he claims that's her natural name, and his own Timber, he regards Timber as a keeper of secrets, which is not natural in a dog.

A flock of blackbirds rises out of the grass and swirls counterclockwise silhouetted against the sky.

It suddenly occurs to Drew that the man who wants to be god just wants to be good with nothing, the freestyle stroke of his swimming thoughts is enraging, and he moves on to the next peg, hammering at it ferociously but to his embarrassment it goes into the ground without any resistance, no roots no trees no trees no breeze, he thinks, even the perpetrators of violence find their own violence intolerable eventually because violence alone is never sufficient, it must always be accompanied by self-denial.

Big day, long journey, returning to camp, Lola locks her bicycle to a pole, perhaps it marks a claim, she looks around.

Quindlan takes three photos, tick tock tick, time but there's not enough of it, the great rivers are powder, the owner pulls the curtains down over the windows to indicate that the business is done.

5

Carolina-Francesca Fornetti has been resigned to her responsibilities for so long that when she takes them up these days she does so in a non-human state, but still she's quite aware, among the humans on board in a shipshape world there are cats and rats, and the situation that develops commands attention.

Her mother was beautiful.

Outside the windows, the world moves again a little—the moment is dreamily little, absurdly small—through wrinkles.

Then bellowing disturbs Carolina-Francesca Fornetti, to waken gradually is normal, one wants to visit a town before buying a house there or burning it down, how ridiculously life continues.

Its rings are chains, yes, but its transitions outlast sequiturs.

Lola waves as she goes by.

In the basket hanging from the handlebars Lola has books, three children live alone in one, a woman sets geese to guard her secrets in another but she's written them down so it's paper not secrets that the geese are to guard and the secrets get about.

Lola is conscious of fiction and therefore of chapters, she knows that things happen, things happen to her, chapter.

Chapter Two

I'm exhausted, says Ludmilla Kaipa, I feel like a lunatic who's stayed out too long in the sun, she shakes her shawl and it's not a simple shawl, her fingers are as sticky as raisins and her fingernails, thinks Fred, are as sweet.

That would surprise Ludmilla Kaipa.

Sid steps out of the gun shop, Fred's Firing and Crackery, onto the sidewalk with a box of ammo in a bag, guaranteed to produce confusion, thrill, and dismal aftermath, there's a range up the hill half a mile back.

The possibility for violence will always get realized, sooner or later, says Fred, do you approve, asks Teddy Mark Mason in his khaki outfit who has drifted out of the afternoon's incoming fog, I don't and I do, Fred says, and that's the truth, which is more than you'll get most people to admit, even to themselves, if and when they talk to themselves, as I'm not ashamed to tell you I sometimes do, especially in my sleep, Fred adds, I treasure sleep I'll tell you, I'll share my bed but not my sleep even if I could, which I can't, so the point's moot, or mute, or whatever, like … Ludmilla Kaipa!

Ludmilla Kaipa, says Fred coming to the door holding an empty brown rifle, Memo stops to stare, Dolores goes on by.

It is possible for someone to be blinded by another's charm, it is also possible for one to be blinded by one's own.

What to See in Chapter Three

Faces everywhere.

Faces bend to the soft valley without emotion except that of ended joy.

The young Marine Sid thinks, he can't see beyond faces, there's nothing behind them, he thinks, he thinks of loud stormy nights and grasses, the sand and dead mice, the battlefield, the population, a lost purse, a dark vehicle.

The young Marine keeps his words in his cheek, he thinks, he's nothing himself but a face at the doorstep with nothing behind him but trees perhaps hiding the sky, why would trees go to such extremes as to hide the sky, in the forest they are trooped with their fellows.

That one feels oneself to be an unworthy person doesn't warrant one's opting out of being human altogether.

The young Marine thinks, nothing follows.

Sid the young Marine has crimson circles on his cheeks like permanent marks of embarrassment or of excitement too long sustained.

Chapter Let In

Someone always comes along to punish the entertainment for hiding the fact that it's real.

Wait, says Graciela Parker, guys, Jeanie Jones says, what, Graciela Parker says, we need a password, Memo says, shoot.

Tiny Toscano appears suddenly over the bushes in the air, Dolores points up at Tiny, there's a long ascent, Quindlan gets her in.

Chapter Inside

My dog Pépé, says Helen, stands midway between society and nature, he's not standing at all, says Maggie glancing at the white dog on its back like a cat kicking its paws in a patch of sunlight on the floor, think of all the laborers and all the labor that takes place between the breezes blowing over the cocoa beans and we who are eating these candies, says Helen, you're the only one eating them, says Maggie, immediately regretting the implied criticism, well it's true of anything we eat, we wouldn't have it without work.

Sometimes people can't resist letting others catch a glimpse of the really awful thoughts that cross their mind.

Helen proposes a toast to all the workers who do all the work and rises to do hers.

The more one thinks, the more passionate one becomes, Helen says.

Helen rubs at the dishes with a red and white cloth.

Chapter Between

With éclat, Lola bicycles into the present moment, four cumulus clouds overhead holding their shape drift north in the blue as is often the case in May and it's May, outside pedal down Lola circles Jeanie and Pinto.

Happiness is never pure, it always involves some sort of renunciation, Lola circles Jeanie and comes to a stop.

Their meeting, like the conjunction of shrubs and the sun, casts a phantom figure on the ground, they look at it and move it on, bumping it over yellowing weeds and a wooden fence, Jeanie Jones has lost her little pink plastic purse.

Nowhere in a dollar bill belonging to an adult is there even a trace of memory, but that's all her dollar is to Jeanie Jones, a small plastic horse and a candy necklace, these are in the pink purse too, a piece of junk that Pinto threw while Jeanie slept into the trash, he can't tell Jeanie that, Pinto regrets.

Lola and Jeanie continue along studying the ground, Pinto tells them to give it up, it's time to get home, he thinks it may not be too late to get it back.

Chapter Aside

Along comes a black hat blown and buffeted around by the wind with no head to hold it up, no eyes to show it the way, a purple ribbon trailing behind.

It's all relative, says Bill.

How sad! Drew replies.

Hands at her sides gripping the bench, Graciela Parker pleads, exclaiming We *can't* leave before the end!

Tony laughs inattentively, stroking his leg, looking down at Graciela, but that was, he says, the end…and you're cold, Nina says.

Nina Lee likes to be in control, she likes to please, she gains control by pleasing.

Yes, well, says Quindlan, coming along in a handsome gray shirt, we are here and these are our times!

Graciela Parker spots Jeanie Jones and with money for Cokes from Tony goes into the dark after her.

Little Graciela Parker is inadequately wedged into chronological time, now she's been knocked loose.

Chapter One

Pinto with his usual naïveté says, if one won everything from everybody for too long, one would have to give back a good part of it in order to begin the game again.

Old Carolina-Francesca Fornetti has eggs in her basket that she's carrying so carefully you'd think them her own clutch, what she produces these days are like the progeny of her physical harmony with the world, if you're a leader among women, she says to Maggie, you'll be called "what's her name."

Shouting breaks out, what are you trying to pull?, you some sort of sicko?, you're such an asshole you can't produce anything except what comes out of your butt!

There's to be a clever rope trick, blue forget-me-nots, sow-bugs, a situation.

Chapter for Fun

Frankie is romping and Fredo is watching, then vice versa.

Chapters intensify everything, chapters express "intensification," Frankie, says Fredo.

Fredo likes the way hurdles come and go, Frankie feels a slight dilation.

Frankie jumps over a sawhorse like sunlight just coming over treetops and shining into a field showing its clover.

Lion or lamb, says Fredo, Frankie says, lamb, Fredo puts up his hand, what we do by chance one day may soon become a habit.

The life of a weed is not an embarrassment, says Frankie.

Chapter Two

Sally Dover and Donald Dover make love competitively, Sally caressing his neck, he caressing hers harder, they outdo each other with the pleasure they offer and the pleasure they express, and when it's over Sally Dover is angry.

Narrating her life to herself at the moment she thinks, she lies not with her lover but with her love, but she's disappointed by the event, she now denies her disappointment and blames Donald Dover for blaming his on her malady, an affliction of the hips or wrists that causes her pain which varies but is never entirely absent, it sometimes lodges in her lower back and goes to her toes.

Sally Dover knows that she and Donald Dover are spoken of separately, they have not resolved into an entity, Sally and Donald Dover, which gives her a degree of satisfaction, a sense of clarity, she hasn't a thought in her head that doesn't come from some book, and all those she has read on her own, sometimes in secret.

Sally Dover is not stupid, but her every attempt to think brings on metaphors and clichés.

Point of View of Chapter Two

Every child should have a dog to call his or her own, every dog should heel, sit, and somersault on command, every dog should beg and count to three, every mother should have a child who does the same, the ranks swell and then diminish, citizens sigh.

Askari Nate Martin takes a ghostly interest in Maggie Fornetti, he wants access to her past—her childhood games, how she scribbled in her workbooks, the source of the scar on her shin, the memento vivi of Maggie Fornetti.

Chapter Two or Three

Education should provide us with more than merely material for justifying our opinions, says Maggie.

Our crimes, you mean, says Nate.

Chapter Three

In the making of any ring there's not one point but three—a pole, another pole, and a quivering figure moving as if along a wire suspended between them—and if the figure as if on a wire falls as if from the wire, it's still part of the ring.

An angry or threatened squirrel taking up a sheltered position on a branch of a solitary redwood, the last standing on this side of town, refusing reconciliation, releases volley after volley of chatter, which Lola in later years will remember as a half-forgotten sound, it never says (it never *can* say) too much.

Wilbur Joliet Cluster, the brigadier on tour, enters the Nest 'N' Egg Café with his entourage, Phil John Twitchell in white, Joe Sanguinetti in blue, Teddy Mark Mason in khaki, and in lilac and cream, Clara Cluster, the bus door closes behind the driver Jesse Brown who steps into the grass, he has brought his lunch and will eat it as usual with a bottle of milk on the ground in the shade.

The white sheets of the sisters Hertha are hanging out to dry, the sisters Hertha like, they say, the afterscent of sun.

Camus on the grass somersaults, tumbling like a soldier's hat blown across a northern California small town battlefield.

Chapter One

Nina Lee is not the sort to change her name as everyone who knows her knows when she married Tony she did not become Mrs. Parker, nonetheless for eleven years Nina Lee has very much liked to say "we three," and by that she has meant herself and Graciela, who is Graciela Parker but whom Nina has felt secretly to be truly Graciela Lee, and Tony Parker, who is drawing closer with a grocery bag and thinking of bees and queens and Sally Dover, his daughter's teacher.

Sally Dover, Tony Parker thinks, would be one of those who go to the well to poison it.

Nina Lee is dressed in green, Tony Parker looks like a first class aviator, the standing white cloud overhead looks like a woman of daring proportions.

Sally Dover has penalized Graciela for writing her book report on Lyn Hejinian, a minor writer, says Sally Dover, in fact unknown, I've never heard of her, and the examples are obscure, C.

Lyn Hejinian is not unknown, what's Sally Dover's problem, Tony Parker says to Nina Lee, Lyn Hejinian is bourgeois and sentimental, she's patently predictably liberal, but at least, Nina Lee says, it's to her credit that she regrets this without tears, hmm, says Tony Parker, Graciela worked hard on this, and though the casting of blame is thought to set things on the way to their end, this isn't the case.

But life is not, Askari Nate Martin is thinking, a given as reality is.

Chapter One

The lungs, heart, liver, bladder, glands, and brain—the very organs of Quindlan think.

Quindlan cannot think of his pleasure in thinking without quivering.

The sensation is this, says Quindlan to Dr. Paloma Klein, I get dizzy, it's as if there's fog in my lungs, and my heart is empty, I don't run a fever.

That's nothing viral, says Dr. Paloma Klein, it's quite mechanical.

Quindlan likes the speed with which she's thinking.

Chapter One

It is late afternoon and Lola goes with her shadow.

Two wagging caravans are crossing the horizon, one approaching, the other moving away, and as the one arrives the other disappears, both are like giants wallowing in years, some taken from others, leaving this one, the difference.

Sue minus Sid is suction, 1999 minus a mere flick is the 21st century, the hours Ludmilla puts in at the shop minus the hours for which she is paid are the hours that turn a profit.

Yesterday minus today, a movie tie-in minus geography, desire minus ivy—but let's look on the plus side, says Maggie Fornetti analytically to Helen, who has buttered her baked potato abundantly and is now dipping a forkful of it into a dish of mayonnaise.

If a cow were to be paired with a bird the result would be sterile but beautiful perhaps, says Helen, but there's no way back from beauty to usefulness, says Maggie.

Helen's lover Sam says, My lover resembles a house.

In the distance a train whistle blows, Mrs. Fornetti says, my daughter is more perfect than the finest melon or the daintiest birch or rooftops in Lisbon, the past does not return.

Chapter One

Heather Hertha is hanging laundry in a backyard where her sister is at work also, weeding and occasionally cleaning the trowel by knocking it on the side of her shoe.

Sally Dover hurries by, she's determined and grim, peace, says Donald Dover, is way better than getting shit done, to Sally Dover.

From somewhere on the street shouting erupts, clowning around, you think what's-her-name has balls?, then pull them out of her panties for players to throw.

The hillside's spoiled perfection brings on sorrow then indignant rage and then sorrow again, each in turn, her hand on a plump roll of her belly, Helen blames herself.

We must prove that the sky is all one thing, says the brigadier Cluster to Clara, Teddy, Joe, and Phil returning, rising from the shaded weeds Jesse Brown thinks to himself, but more than one sky is possible.

Thinning the light, muting the colors of the buttercups and oatgrass and clover, casting a chill, the fog is beginning to come back in.

Chapter Two

Like a shopkeeper's daughter with high aspirations reading her first "grown up's" book Maggie Fornetti sits in the library with a dictionary on her lap, near implausible she finds imperil, on the table before her is *The Iliad*, she spots plays within plays everywhere in it.

She reads, "I sought the war" and "seize the whip and snatch the guiding rein."

Maggie Fornetti is irritably failing to find a theme to which she can give herself over, she cannot demystify the authority of Askari Nate Martin as he remains silent.

Maggie Fornetti considers cutting her hair short, with her fore and middle fingers she mimics scissoring nine inches off.

"Untaken sacks," a theme she can't get over, "not daring to complain."

The "devouring dogs and hungry vultures" will conclude.

Chapter Three

Nina Lee fears that she has faked her selfless generosity, her sturdy dependability, her cheerful eagerness, her charming lack of ambition, her resilient agreeability, true, she is a copy, she thinks, a counterfeit, a falsification, the originals of which abound like indestructible local weeds on the periphery of the campground trampled all day by people trooping through, fearfully Nina Lee soldiers on, she fidgets.

I'm not wearing my watch, Nina Lee says tentatively, glancing surreptitiously toward the empty yellow bowl on the table into which Tony usually drops the car keys.

From somewhere in the distance comes the smell, very much like that of peanut butter, of burning rubber.

It's late, says Nina Lee nervously, Tony Parker says angrily, it's too late.

A heavy mottled moth flies through the open window into the middle of the river in the landscape painted on the lampshade and there it remains, it may want its own death, its own transportation.

Where, says Tony Parker, is the screen.

Chapter Three

Come on, Graciela, Jeanie Jones whimpers.

A twig snaps, a car accelerates toward the ocean.

From somewhere in the shrubbery at the edge of the parking lot the singing of the mockingbird unfolds as in a dream continuing day and night—free of fate, since no matter how much seems to happen, nothing actually does.

Period—so there—it's over—fini—the end—come all.

Chapter One

Welcome, there will be interruptions, that can't be helped, we're occupants of a tent now pitched, there are always many players and help is not always on their side.

Lola's on a bike, Helen is a largeness, Bill tumbles backward and jumps to his feet pointing to the parking lot, Nina says she wishes it were a field in which she could pasture a trick cow, you can't train cows says Bill, but Nina remains spontaneously reasonable, on some days she wakes to play placards and on others to play the flute politically and she says, Look, I'm telling you what I saw not what I know, that comes tellingly second.

Players all have second things poignantly in mind.

That's just what I said to my mother the day I was born, says Jeanie.

A juggler attempts to seize everything at the very instant he lets it go, the juggler says the field doesn't leave us, we leave it.

For all the years that my wife will live after me, though I'm dead I'll long to be with her, says Bill.

Lola cycles past.

Graciela Parker is missing.

Chapter Two

On the kitchen table is a pile of books, Maggie chooses two and vows to rise early and read 10 pages of each every morning, she sets them out at midnight and it's now 7:49, the intervening hours have not been a time without conflict.

If Houdini were to return he'd only do so to remind everyone that he'd left, this is what Askari Nate Martin is thinking, and that alone would be remarkable, his being the proof—and memory—of his own death, which denies both the possibility and the impossibility of his being at all.

Maggie is distracted from her reading by the difference between what she's reading and what she wants to say to Askari Nate Martin that he won't understand, driving back up the hill, with cruelty or tenderness, like a magician at a fair, a young woman with a young man.

Maggie Fornetti thinks, Askari Nate Martin's an escape artist, disappearing into darkness, hardness, the harsh culture of awareness reasoning dubious circles.

Maggie Fornetti knows that she's given to stubborn thought and she knows that it's Askari Nate Martin, but though it may sound moment by moment further along in the story, the story's just a stunt, she thinks, a trapeze act, she lets go, flies through the air, is safely caught, he turns away while the troops pass reality along.

Chapter Aside

Like two quiet horses two city parks department tractors stand in the grey-green dune grass, a breeze is passing through the slightly hazy sunlight, two identical yellow cars go by, then a black truck hauling lumber the color of rust.

The way things around here have changed Pinto says to Romo you'd think we've happened into a burglar's den, where odd things accumulate.

The motley generals stepping out from their battlefield tent take up their positions, they are masters from a circus tent erected in a field in a small town park close to a beach at the end of May, they are ready for the mournful revelries appropriate to Memorial Day.

Romo extends his tongue to the tip of his nose and beyond, with more effort he pushes it to the tip of his chin.

Clowns are constantly engaged in the construction of what will subsequently become a fantasy.

Chapter Three Looking Back at One

The non-sequitur, Quindlan is thinking, is going to be misunderstood, he thinks: things that are no longer, no older, no other disappear contentiously brusquely and then are gone entirely, without argument and he cannot prove that he was reading a Russian novel between 9 and 10 in the morning.

"The carriage and horses had long since been taken off, lead onto the farther bank, and reharnessed. The sun had sunk half below the horizon…."

And half an hour later "he did not even remember how formerly, on the strength of similar wretched logical arguments, it had seemed obvious that he would be degrading himself if he now, after the lessons he had had in life, allowed himself to believe in the possibility of being useful and in the possibility of happiness or love."

His fantasy is merely an expression, Askari Nate Martin thinks, a pontifical expression in search of a problem, its own.

Quindlan refuses to recognize anything as a digression, to take a suggestion, to accept a designation.

Quindlan is curious, his imagination is engaged, he's enraged.

But now a couple hurries by with a buggy carrying an infant wailing in the twilight its never-ending desire, no.

The oak leaves quiver, no point, no period.

Desire yes never to the end.

Chapter at the Same Time

A gust of wind washes over the campground, the pale rattlesnake grass quivers, shadows move and sharpen, then disappear.

The passive payers take up lots of spaces, but there are plenty of places for passing payers, and there's something for even the bit-part players.

Sid is climbing a slope, the barbed live oak leaves crackle underfoot.

Pepe sighs in his sleep and farts.

Clara Cluster is adjusting her two fine breasts in her bra.

Tiny Toscano turns her face to the swirling fog, she stands on an outcrop, she takes a deep breath, she's inflating.

Lola stops, steps down, Lola lets her bicycle drop to the ground.

The breeze smells of tree bark, moss, earth, and faintly of baked potato.

Helen's diary is at hand and she begins, Dear Helen, a conversation with herself, which is very much the same as one with God, a swimming large lack of identity.

Two determined blunt orange-trimmed dark-brown beetles attached at the rear tug themselves into the emerging patch of sunlight beside a gray-green pebble and tremble.

Carolina-Francesca Fornetti looks up to the right slightly from a book in her hand whose author says that nature is an indifferent opponent to consider it.

The air in the sunlight smells slightly salty, rank, then grassy, last wisps of fog disappear in the blue of the sky, soft at first but now getting hard.

Askari Nate Martin is enjoying his day off, his thoughts drift, the newspaper falls from his hand, events fold, he dozes.

Eleanor is turning brown.

Sally Dover is folding Donald Dover's clean white socks.

For a nation as obsessed with youth as this one is, Bill Diaz is just saying to Carmen Kandia Martin, but Carmen Martin interrupts, it is remarkable how virulently hostile it is to kids, I've noticed they are generally unwelcome, says Bill Diaz, they are social pariahs, Carmen says, and the schools are underfunded, the teachers are paid shit, Bill Diaz asks, do you want another piece of toast?

Wilbur Joliet Cluster is in the can.

Abdul Tommy Ahmed shifts gears and backs away from the rubble at the edge of the trenches.

Kurt Krackauer, like many other former utopians, is not a mere theoretician, he has many practices, disappointment doesn't sap his energy, disillusionment doesn't curtailed his generosity, but he's more ignorant and more sentimental than he should be, he is writing a hot editorial for tomorrow.

A strange sound brings Nina Lee to the window.

Quindlan checks the clock, he's not yet satisfied but time is on his side, there's more to a man than mere skeleton and brains, something is coming up.

Dolores is arranging glass cats, damp weeds are sucking at Memo's socks.

Close to the front beyond the cyclone fence at the edge of the field lost in mirages, Phil John Twitchell sees Jesse Brown salute an empty bus stationed at least a hundred feet away.

The lingering fog is suddenly incandescent, a luminous haze in the trees, yellow light blazes out of the field, the sun is breaking through.

Camus nips at a marshmallow, then flips it into the air, the trick's to catch it before it falls, Jimmy Toscano snatches it and eats it.

It's just the friendly bump, says Minnie Jones, of a fly against the window, Pinto.

A robin on the grass is chirping, Mrs. Lee is saying, it sounds as if it's asking a question.

Heather Hertha's tea has steeped too long, she sips, it's sour, her cheeks rise and wrinkle, she's unwillingly pursing her lips.

A boy is blowing a single bugle tilted toward the treetops.

Montgomery is putting out peaches in their paper nests where the pears were nearer the strawberries that bring out the peaches' blush.

Timber has lifted his leg and is peeing on Sue's nasturtia.

Sylvia Martinez is at the bedroom window, a yellow early tiger swallowtail flits upward through the leaves past her this high.

Donald Dover feels a headache pulling at his temples, his brain's like a magnet gathering nails spread on a desk just for collecting until it can't take anymore.

A pair of raucous jays flits wildly back and forth through the trees, they furiously plunge and playfully perch, they might console the confused for their bewilderment, they squawk from the margins of an unfocused human gathering.

Leo X. Lee is playing with a rubber band, he pulls it, snaps it, he is stretching it between the legs of an upended chair, he twangs it, Leo X. Lee is feeling elastic, but about that later he's going to be strangely reticent.

Jeanie Jones won't remember this but she's on a chair, reaching for the marshmallows Minnie has sealed in a ziplock baggie on the highest pantry shelf.

Charles is looking at a map, Dora is irritably writing *une carte postale* to her brother in France, she writes, les pavots d'or et les arbres de séquoia sont incroyables ici, but she is just now transfixed by the pay of pavots, it leans, it sags, she knows, her brother will think them inferior to red poppies and olive trees, tant pis.

Sam is pulling up with a load of red bricks in his pickup, Fred is around the corner dusting guns.

Sand wasps are flitting in and out of a dry path through the weeds over minute piles of dust, the sweet scent of bush lupine is drifting in the breeze, like gusts on the shapes of clouds the workings of chance produce change, everyday life takes observing.

How totally at random things happen, Trish is thinking, but this isn't true, it's crazy, Trish says to Tio, Tio is tilting his head to shake back his hair, no, it's a lot worse than that.

Holly Hertha is stopping still moodily thrilling to the morning, it is momentarily dismaying, hard to tune.

Right now, Frankie is saying, Fredo, we're supposed to be meeting Romo, Fredo says, then vamanos.

A dark car accelerates as it's rounding a curve and three turkey vultures rise laboriously from a raccoon carcass at the asphalt's edge.

The scalloped dark leaves of the live oak tree are emerging from the rising fog, which is alight, burning off.

Romo Martinez has a nail pressed against a fence and is raising the hammer with which he'll hit it, with skill, his showmanship is for more than show, it's a sad piece of property but his showmanship won't be thwarted.

Kitchen knives, spider webs, car doors—things are always fighting back in the everyday life of Tony Parker, who's about to hurl gravel at a shoe.

Dr. Paloma Klein is sliding her stethoscope onto a pad of prescriptions slips, this is just to say, she thinks, all blank, with dead, brown leaves under them.

Drew is turning his baseball cap, putting bill to back, Sue cracks a smile at the front of his shirt, outside of a dog a book is man's best friend and inside a book it's too dark to read, that's good, Drew, says Sue.

A yellow glow flickering off the tall grass onto the side of a white delivery van catches the eye of Ludmilla Kaipa, the van, she thinks, looks like a loaf of bread.

Maggie Fornetti lays her hand affectionately on the 730th page of Robbins Basic Pathology, heavy and blue, and twirls a strand of her hair around her left forefinger.

Joe Sanguinetti is wishing that every step he took didn't raise dust, he isn't fastidious, but he's proudly and that's for Joe

Sanguinetti pleasantly military, with a tissue in his left front pants pocket with which surreptitiously under the table to keep his shoes shining.

Teddy Mark Mason is taking his time over pancakes.

Emmy Babcock is adjusting her stride, moving aside, to pass some small wildflowers undamaged, she wonders who will be brought like the once-and-always wounded to the pitched tent near the cyclone campground fence in the distance where the high school band is out for practice.

Something whizzes by, losing air, light.

Chapter Two

Sue feels she has failed as a mother to Sid because he feels he has failed her.

If you're thinking of your mother it's her child she's thinking of, says Dr. Paloma Klein to Sid.

Or of herself, says Sid.

The spell is broken.

Sid's disappointment with the world is incomplete.

Chapter Allowed

Slowly the sky absorbs the fog but the clouds hold their own against the blue.

The resolute flatness of Quindlan's demeanor is twisted like fabric into unresolved inner intensity.

Quindlan proudly refers to himself sarcastically as a specialist.

It should be sufficient, Quindlan thinks, that I do not hold things in the past tense.

Quindlan watches reality for material he can adapt and transpose into his fantasy world, so does Sid.

Chapter 2

Maggie busily dissipates her doubts as to Nate's feelings by writing him a note in which she says nothing of her doubts or of his feelings, she says, I think the fog is in love with the sun, they're in an embrace, but the heat of the sun will soon send the fog on its way, and after that the afternoon will be hot as you'll see me scribbling this hastily before going down the fair hill by the trail through the poppies to the library to say thanks for the CD, see you around, this takes several cold drafts.

She's been here before.

Then quicker than the eye can blink now the trail is just like the trail as it was then but the one after that appears a shade darker.

The dogs up the hill come down their legs lingering.

It's not rare to see a beast flicker.

It's dimly maritime.

Maggie's often hearing the alarm this day she's walking.

This days she keeps her eye on the ground behind her.

The furtive detective is Askari Nate Martin as he leaps into shadows remaining out of view of the inside of the head of Maggie Fornetti just as the late afternoon light's pauses now move on.

He scowls in rage to warm the fingers at least that's an option, an opinion, however groundless.

Look shout the children in the grammar school playground from their swings that cross in the air.

Look out shout the curmudgeons and the charmers to the veering armies they imagine disappearing into the seemingly swarming dusk.

The sky hovers like a nurse over a wounded man putting her mouth to his ear.

It's just like a turkey vulture, thinks Tio Levette, to expect something always to turn up dead.

Not to put it off not to be put off—it's unthinkable to Maggie Fornetti to think that Askari Nate Martin is unobligingly indifferent and so differently obliged to love, she thinks, not Maggie Fornetti.

Chapter Around

The last of the fog is no more than light just visible in the breeze, the sun is up to the trees.

To see it no mere illusion to see that Lola will see!—but she makes only a brief appearance at this time to say irritably that it takes her time to appear.

There are branches no thicker than wires in hand to dance in the lights of what's to come.

There's a little scab on the skin over the clavicle of a man on the beach.

Dang! says a child Lola thinks to call Maria when she wins at Bingo.

Dang! says a general others generally think to call when he wins a war.

Circles, scenes, and conjunctions—no peace.

What a circus!

Chapter One

Most animals die after inhuman suffering and it isn't the whips that are to blame, wherever *they* die they die singing, says Dr. Paloma Klein to Leo X. Lee, who, at the end of a long song and dance, is in her office because of his knee.

That's knowledge, says Leo Lee, like the platform at one end of a tightrope on which the walker can stop and sun, Leo says, a trench, says Dr. Paloma Klein.

Behind the grocery store, Montgomery is watering the parking lot to keep down the dust, he tosses water from the trappings of water and catches a mere flicker.

The wind has dropped, everything falls still, the air is motionless, the light silent, Helen's dog and Bill's—all dogs, and birds, squirrels, wasps, ants—have paused, they have ceased, life desists, everything stops.

Tony Parker has no partner for his inner dialogue, then it's no dialogue at all?

He finds it isn't.

Chapter One

I'm called Sharl, says Charles to Frankie, and this is my wife, Doe-rah

Eagerly Frankie says his name is Frankie but my real name, he says as if he'd only just this moment received it, is France!— and am I right to guess that you're from France—too, as it were?

From Lyons in the West, says Charles, yes.

This is Fredo, Frankie says.

Olla, Fredo says.

The sun is drifting like a tourist through a country market overhead.

We have arrived to escape Lyons, Dora says—everything is dead there, living every day.

Living every day for the person living it should not be a negligible part of a long biographical act, says Fredo to his surprise.

We cannot know the name, says Dora drawing her shawl closer to her chest, of what, Charles asks irritably, of living every day, Dora says.

Then let's call it a circus and admit rings, says Frankie, each as different from another as the minute before noon is from the minute after, which is when, having parted from Frankie and Fredo, Charles and Dora find Graciela Parker lying as if asleep among the poppies Dora's thought to pick from the yard at the edge of the parking lot among the tall gray weeds.

It's against the law to pick those, hey! Helen is shouting, as Dora whimpers, shudders, and screams.

Later she will remember the moment at random as one she would never justly foresee, mournfully, angrily.

Nearby a kid is standing on the rear bumper of Charles and Dora's red rented Dodge scratching OLLEH into the rear window glass.

Lola goes by, fleetingly.

Lola—voilà!

Chapter Three

Askari Nate Martin shouldn't have been awakened soon after noon for something that shouldn't have happened but it did and only a block from his apartment where he had been dreaming until awakened that he was having dinner with Samuel Johnson who was saying, "Invention," as he tore the gristle and gray edges away from the red center of a great slab of beef on his plate just before the phone rang, "is a faculty given to clowns that's not given to cows."

Stepping into the field Askari Nate Martin scowls and monkey to man the scampering sun scowls back as man to monkey the sun fires.

Graciela Parker has been found.

Chapter Aside

We want to piss in brilliant colors, say Montgomery, Bill, and Drew.

Chapter Three

Along comes the author of the crime, which is a passing detail in a mere entertainment.

And yet it's hardly beneath notice.

The clown enters wearing his and her round infantile face, the children scream, their mother weeps, their father stomps out in exasperation.

It's 2:33 pm, things have begun that cannot begin again.

O Denzel Washington! O Douglas fir with drooping boughs! O yogurt! says Nina as if the kitchen table were a child able to respond.

Grief is taken up and it cannot be transmuted into gratitude.

Grief punishes.

It wants to.

Chapter One

Welcome back, players and payers, all coming along, paraders are shapers—shapers, snipers, and chumps.

The paid must participate more than the payers, the paid invent events, they aren't permitted to invent history.

The paid soldier on suddenly it seems their appearances occur without cause, the payers catch them under spotlight with peripheries obscured, payers are always intimate with the loss of their time as well as their money, experience's ghost.

There is for every payer some one act that is the image of his secret or the secret of his coming out of order.

The fog is coming in again and out for a walk in a sundress Ludmilla encounters it and is shaken like a bee dying on a windowsill or an ant defending its anthill, she says aggressively quivering at the checkout stand setting down shampoo and potatoes, fuck, Montgomery is impervious to her abrupt unsmiling pleasantries.

You always get what you pay for, Fredo tells Charles behind Ludmilla and behind him are Helen, Sam, Donald Dover, Trish O'Reilly, and Quindlan.

Helen smiles, mouth open with just the tips of her teeth bared, as if preparing to give life a well-meaning, amorous nip.

Shall we follow?

Boldly!

Chapter Two

Along come Frankie and Fredo, each licking an ice cream cone, Frankie a white one and Fredo a pink, Frankie's nestled in a napkin, Frankie is so fastidious, Fredo says, and they laugh, as they pass little Tiny who is out with her handsome poodle Camus stepping elegantly along on its leash, expressing something of what, to her mind, Tiny has it in herself to possess, but along the route of Camus's parade of Tiny's self-possession, Little Tiny has been teased, she says it's strange, but *to mean* and *to be mean* are nearly the same though they are not really the same at all.

A little further along Leo X. Lee comes out into the light through a curtain hanging over a narrow doorway.

Improvisation, says Leo X. Lee, is all about being in time and on track, ready to wander and ready to shock.

Chapter One

Along come a multitude of little things, illusion's provided with reality and reality with illusion too, a circus whose rings withdraw in disgust, spread doubt, produce warts, night falls, owls call, the moon comes up, the battlefield is lost in mist.

The juggler tosses his pins, his plates spin, behind him the tumbler slips and falls into a soft new warm bent turd just left by the clown pulling up his pants by green suspenders at the edge of the ring.

Quindlan comes in from the dark off guard, he says, What's the big deal? but his hands are shaking.

Chapter on View

The payers are attentive and now fall spontaneously silent as if they've been given precise instructions.

Being eager to please they are determined to be pleased almost bitterly, they await the unfolding of events and then, in their total innocence, the escape from what they will discover others desire, no matter that what others desire lurks in close proximity.

Like long-distance truckers or tourists, the possibility that they will see someone eviscerated or mauled is among their ugliest fantasies, an expression of their greatest sorrow, and a sorry lot they are, says Quindlan, lowering his camera just as Lola comes along.

Lola's cycling by the payers is seemingly coincidental, but no absurdity is impossible.

Lola bicycles into the payers' midst, she thinks, you'd think every payer had hold of a butterfly.

Lola's little red skirt as she pedals by is breezily lifted off her knee.

The scent of fog, tarmac, and jasmine lies in close proximity.

Lola knows that if she had it to do all over again her mother would have called Lola "Lately" or "Jane."

I'm not afraid, Jane, today she would be able to say.

Lately, she could say, I've not been afraid.

Chapter Aside

Reality comprises all that is given, that's what makes it real, this unjustly just all that is given.

Dolores receives a gift—Tio Levette spins his chair and rolls to get it from a vendor of balloons, maps, avocadoes, rubber swords, fairy wands, model planes, and chameleons on strings—of a chameleon on a red string.

Dolores takes it from Tio's glove and calls it Eleanor which extends its flickering tongue into the external world and then hastily withdraws it as soon as it has sampled the exciting currents circulating there.

Memo waves his sword, which he favorably compares to a trumpet.

Placed on Dolores's shoulder, the chameleon turns green and goes flat to watch not what's going on but what's not, yes, it's a nihilist!

So says Tio Levette, and he should know, waving what there are of his limbs, but here comes Sally Dover—hysteria is in the wings.

Chapter Two

Tiny goes out to the swings, there are three, she picks the one to the left, settles into it, pumps.

Tiny Toscano's greed has the primal force of benevolence.

Through the trees to the left is Sid on his mother's porch, to the right is an armored car, and dead ahead high in the air are birds in black.

Most people fail to notice what they do awake just as they forget what they've done asleep, Tiny thinks as Tiny swings.

Chapter Surmised

Battle loses containment, the housewife (as the term is understood) raking cut grass into a pile reconsiders and bats the blades into the wind.

Injustice interrupts and is unhappy in the extreme.

Justice proceeds closely, continuously creased.

Smoke from a barbecue, a brick to which gray mortar is cemented, and some third element which only seems to make sense of the first two.

Askari Nate Martin rubs his hand lightly back and forth over the troublesome area where generally he thinks his kidneys lie.

Eyes on an earthworm would be of little use underground, but why is justice blind, so that she won't know to jerk the scale back no matter what's about to fall into it.

Another Chapter on View

Memo and Dolores teeter between wonder and annoyance.

Memo and Dolores at age 7 and 9 are too young to know how dangerous a cliché can be, how quickly and gratuitously it can kill, it's fun just to be out as if in Amazonia alone except for each other and the chameleon called Eleanor, Dolores has Eleanor in her hand.

Where there was no breeze at all now there is suddenly wind.

Happiness?

Sadness?

Plovers and companionship and information and consul generals.

Many years ago, after his fall, Lorenzo Fornetti's vocabulary changed completely, it shifted, it now existed only nowhere, where he found a meaning for words like roff and mott and pum and slemmy none of which meant Chianti or botanical gardens or Karl Marx or lion trainers, Carolina-Francesca and Maggie and neighbors and doctors ruled those out, he'd stamp in frustration and rephrase what he'd said, in the end the trick wasn't to discover what he didn't mean but what he did and they never mastered it, his words were as magical as a juggler's balls, to hear him talk was spellbinding.

Look, Fredo, says Frankie, I know I'm just being subjective but imagine! if I weren't here I wouldn't be seeing all these—these objects—objectively, or any other way, says Fredo, seen all together from a distance, Frankie says, I bet they'd merge and end up resembling something like a patch of elephant or alligator or rhinoceros skin, and we wouldn't, says Fredo, know which.

Flirtatiously Fredo runs his fingertips up Frankie's thigh with sudden bravado and Frankie jumps as a horse might, it's delightful, he shies.

Litter swirls, the weeds brush against the cyclone fence.

Adieu forest! Frankie says, waving at a band of adolescents who are grouping themselves together to be photographed by a stranger.

Chapter One

Poppies are opening as the fog lifts, the warped hexagons of the sagging cyclone fence come clear, a jay calls from somewhere in the oaks growing in the ruins of the abandoned limestone quarry.

This is the last empire of Graciela Parker.

Lola in her red skirt comes along, she might have gone straight on ahead, it might have been the better course, but she's circling back, the angle between front wheel and frame a mere 10 degrees if that but it's enough to bring her around, through the schoolyard, sheltered by a row of fir trees, their lower limbs sawn off to prevent kids from climbing them.

Energy and sweetness are perpetual antagonists, Fredo says.

Frankie squats, an entirely natural gesture, to tie his shoe, the sisters Hertha stop, Fredo, Helen, and Sam wait with Drew, Frankie hitches his pant leg and everyone erupts in laughter, they cannot stop, tears roll down Fredo's face, the younger sister Hertha shrieks she's "about to pee," they laugh until their faces ache and their souls are perplexed.

Chapter Around

The coldest hour of this particular day occurred in the morning at six, foggy and still, and the warmest at five in the afternoon, gusts of wind from the south moving through the bay trees smelling of pepper in the heat along the shallow creek bed behind the school.

Askari Nate Martin is walking up from the creek, aware of the crunch and scratch of gray pebbles, brittle oak leaves, and dry soil on the path under his footsteps and an echo at the edges, dust clinging to the bottom of his pants.

Askari Nate Martin deals with the detail, the anomaly whose integration into context is required, the particular whose loss he'd mourn as if it stood for all of external reality, as if its loss would leave him with the internal world alone.

Somewhere above and off to the left a woodpecker knocks its beak against a tree and chickadees twitter like crickets incessantly as they flit within the dense shadows amid the branches of the live oak trees.

The heavy creosote-soaked railroad ties laid out to mark the parking spaces in the lot at the entrance to the empty fairground are reeking in the sun.

A scrub jay lands in a manzanita and scolds, then flutters a few feet upward into the branches of a small pine from which it scolds again, emitting (no, transmitting) anguish.

To be is to perceive, he thinks, or to perceive to be.

Chapter Aside

Bill and Tio and Minnie and Sue are reasonably sure that they saw Nina an hour ago making a phone call not long after weeping.

It was just after dusk and it's just the same now, before people have drawn the curtains.

The trail is cold, it's already late but the things that go on are impossible to punctuate.

And to think it all a mere appearance!

To think that we'll see it sink!

The twigs have yet to be settled, they crack underfoot, they refuse to lie undisturbed

Hear what I am telling you I see they say seemingly.

Sid steps furtively into the library at the sight of Helen.

Drew ducks behind a tree at the sight of Mrs. Lee.

Chapter to See

The soldiers run around with their wagging fat flashlights beaming into broad daylight, says Tio Levette, they pile up—a human pyramid!—they will never make it past Chapter One to Chapter Two, or they'll go, says Sylvia Martinez, directly from One to Three, Tio Levette says, always legally.

Chapter One

Why does Sid step furtively into a doorway at the sight of Helen?

Why shouldn't Drew duck behind a tree at the sight of Mrs. Lee?

Chapter Three

Askari Nate Martin sees a great difference between the words "evidently" "apparently" "seemingly" even "probably."

Everything, when he gets down the block to the overgrown weedy ditch has to be taken in.

The field is beautiful but the trees are crouching, some of the shadows are rocking, others are waiting like newborns for a slap or like fledglings in their nest for a macerated worm.

Askari Nate Martin's own shadow thins in the pale radiance of the foxtails, a rusty leaf from a madrone is caught on a gray twig of an oak tree, the ground has been struck a blow, maybe many.

Examination, according to Askari Nate Martin, discloses that each of us, free or not, is a being subject to modification.

Chapter Midway

Sue's house is pocked as if it's been strafed, its flat roof sags from the weight of fallen leaves, yellow, brown, green, black and blasted, Sue's just coming out, she's trying to pull Sid in.

Calm as clockwork, free of meaning, innocent as the scattered moths, guilty as the very fairgrounds in the clear of day on the wrong side of town where one sees the reflection of a face in a shaking lake repeat, Sid breathes.

A bad past has no future, Sid doesn't like things to conclude.

Slant sands, mountains pulling away, a vendor in tawdry—no a merchant in motley—barking his wares, snakes on sticks, yellow rifles, whips, and a bowl of red candies.

Unconscious war offers a running commentary on the flow of conscious experience Sid can't resist.

Tiny at a little distance in the park is watching through her hair, between her feet surreptitiously as she swings, green at a distance marking her chain, her claim, her determined chin with signs, but of these she's unaware.

Camus, arbitrarily targeting a clump of weeds, pees on it and makes it his responsibility.

Sue thinks, my son Sid and I suffer from disconnected modifications of each other we'll never understand as they go in.

Two heavy jays flit boldly back and forth between the branches of two dark oaks, one calls out shaaar, the word descending.

Chapter One

Sharl, Dora flutes, through a small mouth with red lips.

Charles, says Dora, Americans when they think about themselves as they so often seem to do become completely confused.

Americans enjoy being young, says Charles, but of course not like incontinent infants in dirty shirts.

Charles, yes, Dora says, *c'est vrai*, Americans very frequently launder.

Charles, says Dora, Americans smile readily but when they should they do not look away.

The progress of Dora and Charles in their stroll is momentarily impeded by a garbage collector hefting a green can toward a paused white truck, its hydraulic brakes belch.

When Americans let something in they always leave something out, says Charles.

Bill waves, walking Timber.

Every American feels that at the very least American life always has another 100 years remaining, Dora says, poor century, Charles says, yet another, says Dora, they leave Montgomery's Market each biting into an Eskimo Pie.

Chapter Discontinued

Gap: scraping of a rake, sounds like a ratchet or a wheel turning, a tree falling, continents shifting, termites ....

Quindlan shakes—his head.

He cannot advance.

A dog, not far away, shrieks then falls still.

Chapter One Introduces Chapter Three

A crime has occurred in Chapter Three, maybe more than one, that's for Askari Nate Martin to discover, but in Chapter Two Maggie Fornetti considers bicycling past the police station in the hopes of encountering, as if by chance, Askari Nate Martin.

She dismounts.

It is explicable but not necessary that Quindlan happens to take a snapshot of Maggie at just this moment.

Quindlan explains that the photographer's interest is not sincere but neither is it patronizing, it's momentary, random, reactive, he catches Maggie Fornetti with Askari Nate Martin.

Maggie Fornetti is far too human to care for art or is she far too human not to care for art, she knows she can't have it both ways and would like to ask Quindlan what he thinks.

She has a picture that she studies with great delicacy and a violin that she plays without melancholy and no one's bad opinion, she vows, will keep her from satisfying her curiosity, but she is highly susceptible to opinions, these are, to her regret, what she is too often curious about.

Maggie Fornetti must have had a pleasant childhood, she understands very little about human nature.

Chapter Three

At the edge of the creek Askari Nate Martin finds the tracks of someone passing through the scene on bare feet in the mud which is to be kept under observation.

The tracks continue, then reverse, then ramble—the walker seems not to have been troubled by sudden realizations.

He or she does nothing, but shows no signs of inhibition.

From the depth of the tracks in the mud, he or she seems to hurry yet not to have been bossed around, but this is not a solitude, the only solitudes are unwatched.

Here and there against the bank a pool forms, as it were behind the current, or out of its way, no longer relevant, sheltered by a fallen log or sand bar, the water hanging in still air or, like this one, in glare neither admitting nor emitting images, it resembles a metal surface, or a mental one.

It has been the scene of something—a scene in someone's life.

It is Quindlan who complains about "our freedom, our futility, our inability to hide."

Chapter Through

Along come three adult male cyclists sweeping past Lola in brightly colored tight cycling suits bent low over the handle bars, each straining forward as if, Helen thinks, in an effort to escape a body he no longer finds habitable.

Then one leans back suddenly pulling the front wheel off the ground, doing a wheelie, allowing his body to catch up.

His suit is an iridescent green with purple swirls running up the front along one side from his ankle to his neck, then over his shoulder, and down his back and buttock to his ankle again.

He looks like a reptile, Helen thinks, but he can't deny his humanity.

He looks traumatized, but that may be merely prophetic.

Helen's sadness today is becoming militant.

Chapter One

Lola spins into view, scarcely noticed, from within, at the periphery Lola stops, she puts her right foot in its pink shoe on the ground, her hands are on the handlebars, she watches, as if in pain, her eyebrows twitch, grimacing momentarily as a baby does at a digestive twinge, very briefly she frowns.

Memo has a dappled ball that he tosses to Camus who yaps, it's missed and falls into the crowd.

Helen tousles Fredo's hair, Minnie Jones bumps Tio's chair.

Dolores cavorts after two squirrels racing for cover, aggressively they volley chatter, darting into the new action Memo mimics them, he throws weight.

The raising of a flapping flag, aphrodisiac, fun, alarm.

Performers tease observers, observers performers, everyone together is stirring up the sudden violent possibilities of the entire landscape.

Clara Cluster smiles at Teddy Mark Mason in khaki and Joe Sanguinetti in blue.

Familiarity is breaking down the fortifications of conventionality, the distinction between players and payers is disturbed.

Quindlan takes up a strongly defensive posture.

Outside the late afternoon breeze is pushing through the leaves, the acrobatic shadows settle in the trees like snipers.

Chapter One must make an assertion and announce Chapter Two.

Chapter Two

Think your worst thought, Nina Lee says angrily to Tony Parker, think the worst you can imagine.

Tony thinks that thinking itself has turned criminal.

What I think is a secret, Tony thinks, if only it will keep the very existence of itself a secret.

Chapter One

Worries riddle stories, Sally Dover thinks, eavesdroppers might be anywhere, what is the product of oppression?

Buried treasure!

And prisoners in yards ....

More prisoners than guards!

But how do we know what Sally Dover thinks?

No one among the countless hundreds of people because of their very density can move a foot and no one because of the congestion can do anything but stand like a marble statue, immobilized or, as a last resort, screaming.

According to Tony Parker, Sally Dover has hit the roof.

Chapter Three and Two

Askari Nate Martin's secret is that he believes that every crime is committed in the name of love, every love invents a crime to carry out and does so.

Someone should ask Nate, then, if there is happiness in getting away with it, but he has no inquisitor.

What he knows of crime and what he knows of love are much the same, says Carolina-Francesca to whom Maggie is confiding.

The enormous ego of the melancholic Askari Nate Martin is composed of remnants, the sum total his accumulated losses.

In a notebook he expertly sketches multiple horizons, clowns, rivers, spiders, and shifting poles.

In fall the golden orb spiders proliferate, but in May their broken webs are less easy to locate.

It's evening, and Quindlan is taking out the garbage, but as if it were luggage, as if it had angles, as if it came from a bunker, as if it had been composed by Vivaldi.

Sid was never a fire eater, Sue eagerly says to Askari Nate Martin, who knows there are many ways to keep someone from playing.

Chapter Through and Through

The players must accept all the rules.

Can you deny this?

What sort of wretched invention is human language, when it says one thing and means another? asks Carmen Kandia Martin.

Fred asks, who's asking?

To perfectly hear oneself speak, shouldn't one listen from a distance as if to a stranger?

At the beach, says Bill.

Askari Nate Martin asks himself, must every tragedy begin with a bad decision?

Are the good intentions with which Hell's paved, Helen, ones you've dug up to add to a cake?

You say you "interpret things," so do you consider yourself, Sam, a superstitious person?

Chapter Three

Helen feels guilty of her unhappiness and her happiness, Sue of furtive decisiveness, Sue is too ambivalent for calm, she comes to one conclusion and then comes to another, no decision has been made for good, but there's nothing in the ambivalent state that prevents her from feeling vibrant joy or grief, which Sid doesn't notice, if he did he wouldn't be able to adapt it to the reality of his idea of her.

Sue bears the lopsided truth of the phrase "the parent of Sid" without argument, lopsidedly, Helen's weight creases the skirt she sits in.

Chapter Aside

We have each lost a purse, Askari Nate Martin, says Holly Hertha, in less than an hour, Heather Hertha concurs.

Heather, says Holly Hertha, is just like a fortune-teller who can tell other people's future but not her own, Holly, Heather Hertha says, is just like a fortune teller who can tell but cannot see, Holly Hertha adds, mercy.

Things add up, I do the math, says Holly Hertha, with many arms, Heather Hertha says, three by two with one for the remainder, the sisters Hertha say, things add up nicely.

Chapter One

It's as if Askari Nate Martin, ss # 545-09-3825, living at 93 Bennett Rd., son of May and Jackson Martin, telephone number 652-9850, has no identity, and as if Maggie Fornetti, ss # 573-92-7579, living at 27 Pineview Rd, phone number 897-2979, has no identity too, they have no grounds for getting to know or be known, then what is plot without character and what is character without plot.

Askari Nate Martin opens a case and pulls binoculars from its worn magenta lining, he scans the hillside, Askari Nate Martin does not like to be categorized, he does not like to be thought of as a "sort of person," but Helen does.

I'm the sort of person, Helen says to Fredo, who doesn't mind being interrupted though she's just said to Sam that she is the sort of person who does.

When others dislike the place it falls to Helen to like it and she does, or she feels that she does (they're much the same, there can't be any reasonable distinction between liking and having a feeling of liking), but the others today seem jolly in their disliking while she today in her liking is morose.

Chapter Three

People are frightened, says Bill, meaning that he is, but he says it in a sarcastic tone, disguising his meaning.

Far away but not far enough away the shouts of a battle continue, explosive cursing, an uproar.

The future is blocked, nothing can change, regret is irrevocable.

Come, astronauts envious of lumberjacks, come, piano tuners desperately humming A, come, political aspirants gnawing buttered corn, come, Pépé, come back.

No one comes forward, Askari Nate Martin is waiting, can animals hope that things will be peaceful day after tomorrow, are the soldiers in the alley jovial, someone has fallen, Timber howls.

Chapter Three

Sally Dover cries, The cash box has been plundered.

Would this continue if there weren't guns of war thundering at the door?

Everything, says Quindlan, is mere continuation when there's more to come.

Sally Dover calls the children to attention, even the bruised one, Jane, the best speller.

Helen says, many come in and all go out before.

Like a figure shot from a cannon on his way to the beach from the bank black helmet tight on his head, Bill on his motorcycle speeds by.

Every gun is a gun of war, says Maggie Fornetti, lifting her backpack, pulling at her hair.

Anxiety is brought on by the disappearance of desire, Quindlan says, the other you've desired has come too close.

Chapter Three

Around powerful people Quindlan feels at ease, he lets his disdain circulate, he lets his anger develop, he gives in to admiration, without the anxiety he feels when it's he who's the object of (malevolent) praise or (manipulative) solicitude, rising from the Nest 'N' Egg table he leaves a paltry tip without a word.

Chapter for Now

There are two captains for now, three sergeants, two interpreters, 24 men, and a dog in front, then racing to the side, barking in the distance, scampering back, jumping out of the ditch, he's brought under control.

The troops prepare to reenact the taking of a hill across modified terrain in the heat of composition its hills have disappeared.

The squad on bulldozers deploys, whirling cones of dust rise in their wake, Pinto, puffing, puts himself in their path, he points, he protests, they are advancing on a nest.

Isn't it a bit late for Pinto to be jumping onto the be-kind-to-animals bandwagon, says Leo X. Lee irritably to Tio Levette, who is turning off the boom box he carries on his lap in frustration, every goddamn fucking bandwagon is all about fucking blaring and that's all they're about, Tio says, fucking bandwagon blaring.

A killdeer feigning injury goes up the road and down again.

History's flattened.

Chapter with Nothing Won

Lola circles a tree, dead leaves cracking, breaking under the wheels, she steers for a row of pitched brown tents, a group of soldiers dodge, she glides, she's pulling a stunt, there is going to be a parade.

Chapter to View

Along comes the mayor of the town Pinto Jones with his wife in her blue jeans, Mrs. Minnie Jones, and their cheerful daughter Jeanie, whizzing past is Lola, a cyclist, age 9.

Keeping a croissant from Pépé whom she's carrying along comes Helen who is very large with her lover Sam.

Suspiciously along comes Quindlan wearing a grey-green shirt.

Along comes Bill from the bank jovially in suit and boots, Guillermo Diaz, with Timber tugging on his leash.

Detective Askari Nate Martin comes along, striking as in a poem, "will the machinegunners please step forward," he's pessimistic.

Along comes Graciela Parker's mother Nina Lee who is filled with desires none of them her own and along comes Graciele Parker's father who is angry, Tony Parker.

Graciela Parker is no enemy of life, but there will be no more of Graciela Parker.

Along comes old Mrs. Lee, she had a parakeet but let it go, weakening around the ears and knees, with Leo X. Lee, a fidgety musician, the younger brother of Nina Lee.

Along comes Dr. Paloma Klein, and the sisters Hertha, and the owner of the town bar, Drew, and along comes Emmy Babcock, the principal of the new low stucco school.

Jimmy Toscano is coming along reluctantly kicking at weeds, he bobs ambiguously at Fred feeling thwarted, maybe Jimmy Toscano's being kept at or keeping his distance, he swats at a bee and goes off to the right.

Fred comes along with a silver dollar in his pocket shot through the middle, the personal bull's-eye he'd like to show to Tiny, along she comes.

Trish O'Reilly comes along, having nothing better to do.

Tiny Toscano is a lovesick girl, says Trish O'Reilly to Montgomery and Drew, to her way of thinking if houses turned into horses she was given to ride it would be nothing near as wondrous as the return of Sid, Trish says, there's nothing a teenage girl does better than to sit around and stew, but Tiny's being pulled along by the beautiful poodle Camus, front legs in the air, so along she comes.

Teddy Mark Mason and Phil John Twitchell are mildly pissed off that they've got to come along

No coming along can surprise Clara Cluster, Clara Cluster's good at granting concessions, she feels it is noble to do so, she is pettily nagged by her nobility, for just a moment she is just coming along with Joe Sanguinetti.

Thinking of how later to roast the pork in the fridge, along comes Donald Dover, just leaving his office like a dog out of a darkroom, with cabbage perhaps, or figs.

Wilbur Joliet Cluster, the brigadier with beaming one-star status, comes along with his eyes to the sky, always looking to the future, making history ass-backwards.

A sparrow sings twice from the crown of a shrub, Jesse Brown comes along as announced, goldfinches swoop off the thistles.

Like something that's lost consequence and is now to be given away, Sid the young Marine comes along like the best sweater of someone who's dying quietly with his mother Sue.

Along come Sylvia Martinez, a lawyer, and Romero, and here come the children, Romo, Sylvia Martinez says, here are Dolores with her ill-fated chameleon and Memo with Tio Levette, their uncle propelling his wheelchair, he is turning to say something to Ludmilla Kaipa.

Along comes Sally Dover, keeping her distance from the weeds for fear of ticks.

Carolina-Francesca Fornetti comes along alone now that Renzo's gone.

Along comes Carmen Kandia Martin, one of the teachers, Askari Nate Martin's sister, with Maggie Fornetti, Askari Nate Martin cares no more for me than a horse does for pasta primavera, Maggie Fornetti is thinking.

Along comes Abdul Tommy Ahmed who works in the lumberyard, Kurt Krakauer, and Montgomery who's the butcher from the grocery store, the gay Fredo and Frankie, and along comes the couple from France who call themselves "Sharl" and "Dor-AH."

Through the population to whom histories come around around again comes Lola.

Chapter Three

The most basic and urgent of a child's needs are survival and pleasure, and maybe pleasure is subservient to survival, says Emmy Babcock to Minnie Jones toward the end of the day, to guarantee those, says Carmen Kandia Martin, children need power.

Sally Dover calls some children away from the gap in the cyclone fence separating the yard from the sluggish small creek on whose shallow almost stagnant water water striders stride, a robin flies out from the shadows of an oak silently.

She's there in a flash to cast a grim light, that's Sally Dover all over, says Emmy Babcock, removing the lid from a tin of jellybeans and offering one to Minnie Jones.

Graciela Parker is too young to understand burial, too young to be exposed to cremation, everyone now has the unpleasant task of explaining to themselves to little Graciela Parker that she's dead.

Chapter Two

Several quail forage through the poison oak into the foxtails, kicking bits of dirt and leaves left and right in search of seeds, head plumes bobbing, Carolina-Francesca Fornetti draws a deep breath.

Carolina-Francesca Fornetti in considering an opinion memorizes it, she thinks, she aspires to be opposed by nature's indifference.

A cannon fires, the sound echoes roundly, things die away.

Carolina-Francesca watches the ripples stirred on the surface of language just legible on the gravestones, the incantadas.

Carolina-Francesca accepts the death of Lorenzo Fornetti so completely that she can't remember what he was like nor what she was like when, if ever, he was alive, she thinks, to me.

My flesh is flabby, Renzo, Carolina-Francesca says to the grave, how can anyone have self-respect left like this.

The ground is still warm, warm air rises from it, as cold fog swirls high overhead.

Carolina-Francesca is suffused with the same deep embarrassment, the overwhelming shame, that, sweeping over her like rising orchestral music, wakes her night after night, she wants to know, what have I done, is this self-pity, she's thinking, sterility?

Off goes a fusillade.

Chapter One

Tiny dislikes her brother so much that to think of him is the same as thinking of her dislike of him, it oppresses her, it dampens her spirits, she dislikes him all the more for that, for being so dislikable, and she dislikes him too for being so disliked.

Here, says Jimmy, are the two filched purses.

So!

The passive payers take up lots of spaces, but there are still plenty of places for any passing payers, and there's someplace always to be found for even the merely bit-part players.

You see?—there's dramatic footlighting yet to be seen and psychological backlighting, the action can be perceived sometimes as real, sometimes as battle, sometimes as merely imagined, every encounter reflects others and every encounter anticipates that another is coming along, high-wired, trammeled, pitched, or clowning around.

Where there's sibling rivalry, there's sibling revelry, where there's a memorious reveler with boom box blasting there's a polyglot talker, where there's a squad of stilt-walkers there's someone mired in a nightmare running at a snail's pace, fruitlessly.

It's all, for Tommy Ahmed, in a day's work, the ends of a hundred wet two-bys on the ground raw and red, while Sid like a payer from the slow-moving depths of privacy looks on, the banners blow.

Chapter Two

Askari Nate Martin has quickly set up his desk and is sitting looking at the photographs, the image has no name except metaphysically, he's distracted, he has that in focus, Maggie Fornetti.

It has occurred to Carolina-Francesca Fornetti that over the years one spends with one's lover if one is lucky enough to have years and lucky enough to spend them with one's lover the image of the lover in one's mind drifts out of focus, she can't now securely place Lorenzo Fornetti's face.

A cat stalks a bird, the cat leaps and misses but creates a moment for itself, that's what time is—the rupture called failure that even for a cat is an event.

Chapter Taken By Surprise

The General leaves an ugly dark bird in the pool of the portable outhouse, it bobs, in due time, it will turn into a swan, the General emerges with dignity, the General is not in mufti.

The warmth of the sun is rising from ground and moving out under the incoming swirling fog.

Chapter One

It is occurring to Joe Sanguinetti as it has to Pinto Jones that there might be an outpost back of town in the woods, he pats his back right pants pocket and is reassured to feel his wallet, there you are says Clara Cluster, have you seen the General.

Trish O'Reilly comes out of the bank wearing high-heeled shoes as yellow as buttercups atop quivering stems, she adjusts her little white purse strap over her shoulder and stumbles naturally, Trish O'Reilly grabs Phil John Twitchell's outstretched hand.

Fade, blackout, snap on, the lights flicker.

It's obvious that Phil John Twitchell is not oblivious.

Payers and players alike are spurred to action.

Chapter Aside

Along comes a wheelchair for two carrying four with enormous heads, mouths open, three laughing and one screaming.

The miser cannot come along, he's paralyzed by his hoard, impervious to catcalls, ululation, and screams, he's running rings without knowing how senseless the point he's circling is, it's the dried out counterpoint to the miser, the miser can never have a last word and it's not he who left the turd.

The turd is someone else's work as are the products lit by bulbs that brought the miser his gold and the conviction that he has the right to say as he cracks his whip and the lions roll over, man is simply amazing!

Chapter Two

All gets subsumed back into the structure of which they're parts of the day, the crime, the town, the war, and this.

For a few minutes there walking with Askari Nate Martin without speaking Maggie Fornetti feels she is being for once completely understood.

Wait, Maggie Fornetti says, there's a foxtail in your sweater, Nate hesitates, pauses, Maggie lifts the back of his green sweater with her left hand at the ribbing and pushes the foxtail through with her right, see?, they continue and see Sid coming out of the shadow of Drew's shop hefting a green backpack onto his shoulders.

Sid's a sweet guy, says Maggie, with secrets, Nate says, they hold him back.

Chapter 2

If your skin were canvas I'd paint on it, if the canvas were your skin I'd sleep inside it, says Askari Nate Martin.

Maggie Fornetti flings her right arm to the side and then above her head.

Maggie Fornetti sprawls.

She's representing herself to herself, representing body to mind, but she doesn't represent the external world to herself, she doesn't represent to herself herself in the external world, to do so would be to acknowledge the inevitability of losing the world.

And from far away in his haunting account Askari Nate Martin crawls, a subject represented to itself as a failure in what's therefore, in Maggie Fornetti's view, a failed representation as she finds him as finely presented fine.

Askari Nate Martin is mapping, three two one, one two three, he practices a melancholic science, as do astronomers, archeologists, and navigators.

He draws back.

As the spots of ink spread, colors form at their fringes.

What I think of you changes by the inch, Nate says.

The imposition of objectivity upon the world between them flows.

Maggie lifts a shoulder, turns, points her toes.

Just then, Askari Nate Martin says later as they linger before they part reminiscing, your past and my future fused, as in a surrealist fantasy or, he adds, a nightmare, offending Maggie Fornetti suddenly, whose possible loss he is already mourning.

Chapter One

Quindlan's ivory tower is low to the ground, he's as shortsighted as a dung beetle that thinks everything is after *his* pile of shit, says Tony Parker.

Quindlan screws the camera onto the tripod and adjusts its several rings.

At the end of the day, as the school's doors open, out come educated dogs, says Quindlan, boxing elephants, and no doubt some future star of a human 'iron jaw' act trained to dangle from the heights.

Day after day inch by inch his photographs remain silent.

A marshal in the field, a sharpshooter in a clown's hat, a roadside ditch at the edge of which lies a toy didgeridoo.

At some point in every photograph something of the dark of night is admitted.

Now we'll go from Chapter One to Chapter One Two.

Chapter One Two

Teddy Mark Mason is running his fingers along the crease of his cap, pinching, it's beige, as Jimmy Toscano comes along, isn't that what you guys call a cunt cap, says Jimmy, he's got his hands in the pockets of his coal black hoody.

Spiffy.

Phil John Twitchell admires the trees.

I imagine, says Joe Sanguinetti, that the bark would fly off in chunks, Phil says, maybe, the trunks are pretty much the color of old dry blood.

Teddy Mark Mason says, I like their pitch.

Jimmy Toscano takes his right hand out of his pocket and twice punches the bus, Jesse Brown marches up.

A yellow butterfly flits by, a woodpecker taps somewhere high on the trunk of a live oak tree hidden among the leaves.

Chapter Three

Not precisely at 3 but five minutes later Detective Askari Nate Martin arrives at the low ochre school to speak with Sally Dover.

Askari Nate Martin detects with the perceptivity and flexibility of a lover or a cardplayer.

Older kids, says Sally Dover, are always badgering the little girls, a fact Emmy Babcock confirms, and why report it, Sally Dover asks rhetorically, it's nothing new, children's cruelties, which, says Emmy Babcock, just add to children's anxieties.

Sally Dover's is not a classroom that looks hastily improvised, the twenty-two used paper cups were neatly stacked before being dropped into the trash, and not every child has artwork on the wall, Graciela's is of a blue birthday cake with 1 green, 2 pink, and 5 red candles burning beside a long-tailed yellow animal facing out.

Sally Dover can always find a way to justify her actions and persuade herself that she is right, she does it in the pretense of "offering clarification."

Things shown the door tend to return through the window, Sally Dover says, wiping off the surface of her desk with a piece of floral patterned dampened paper towel.

Dropping Chapter Three

In the quiet Tony Parker weeps still.

Dead in a still life, thinks Askari Nate Martin, to whom invaded interiors are old news.

Quindlan is not dead to the implications.

With equanimity, Quindlan might have trusted to fate, but it's his own decisions that bring him to the present moment.

The sensation of having a bad conscience is as narcissistic as the sensation of having a good one.

Helen takes her tray of cakes toward Nina Lee and Tony Parker like a vendor, everyone eats, says Helen.

Quindlan turns, he is pale, he says yes.

Chapter 2

Askari Nate Martin anticipating pursuit thinks of Achilles pursuing the tortoise in Zeno's paradox as in a dream, the pursuer never succeeds in catching up with the fugitive whom he is after and the fugitive can never escape his pursuer, he thinks, Maggie Fornetti.

Maggie Fornetti wakes early this last morning of May, colors scattered in the slow reality of light.

Two cats are contesting loudly yowling, one basso the other profundo, a pair of doorbells angrily pressed by police thumbs it seems, a dream.

Maggie sits up.

It's not other people I pay attention to but my relationship to them, all my thoughts are for what's between us, Maggie thinks to herself, an admission that she hopes without saying so to herself will improve this relationship, the relationship of Maggie Fornetti to Maggie Fornetti.

The sun has not yet come over the hill but it's getting lighter.

Emmy Babcock embraces Minnie Jones with tears in her eyes, Minnie cries.

What can we do? what have we done?

Chapter After Chapter

What have you remembered, children, Sally Dover asks, the war, and the wounded, and the dead, they say, and cattle sent to slaughter, says Jeanie Jones, and Graciela Parker, good lord, Emma Babcock says, Sally Dover's going over the top.

Chapter One

If this were a novel, on the first page it would have begun and on the last it would be done, but something or someone always comes along.

The chapters do but are never done.
Chapters Three and Two and One.

Chapter One

Grief takes time, they say—it takes it all.

It devastates way stations, obscures patterns, and flattens balls.

A consequence of any action should be a memorizing of it (however furtive, brief, partial, reconfigured, or frequently interrupted).

But no action of Nina Lee's killed Graciela Parker, there is nothing of it to remember, she cannot think about Tony Parker—his right forefinger, his tears, the cereal on the floor, the dented fender of his car.

Lola lets her bicycle fall to the ground and walks up to the door.

Chapter To View

A novelist is no more a scientist than a snake charmer is a herpetologist or a tightrope walker is an engineer or a cook is a chemist or a voting booth is a sanctuary or a confession is an autobiography or the folding of the nomad's hammock is a surrender of territory.

A goldfish is no more a guard dog than a divorcée's guilt is a balancing rod in the hands of the tightrope walker making his or her way from the Arctic to Antarctica or vice versa.

Go, little pebble, go shoe, go accountants in trances, go missionaries distributing rice to saxophone players on tour in the Sierras, go naked.

The lion in its cage knows that life's a preposterous catchall.
I'll sleep here tonight, says Nate Martin.
Sawdust and circular reason.
Chapter Three done, Chapter Two, Chapter One.

Saga

The Distance

I

Banned from ships as if I were fate
Herself I nonetheless long hankered after adventures
At sea
But buckets, lifeboats, gulls, and fish guts on wharves were as near
as I got
Or the beach. The ban was inoperative on the sands and there I
boarded
Wrecks, where the terns, godwits, and gulls were ashore
As at sea and from beaches
I observed the fine points by which one can distinguish
Between the sandpipers
Just as I learned that there are many fine points to fate
Which divulges what comes to pass indefinitely
So that we can hardly say of things that happen that they were
meant to be
Or that they weren't. Like a pupil
I was ruled by obedience
To rules I broke. I floundered around
And enjoyed my choices—I was eager
To receive—
But not without perplexity. I was endowed with doubt
And that is one of the few things I can say of myself then
That I can say of myself
Now, for the most part there has been little confluence. I've been
swept
Against objects, lost habits,
Knowledge grows
But it has to be connected to things.
That connection is usually best achieved
So they say
Through perceiving similarities. No way!
Winds blow in a giant circle and set up resistance to anyone
Going the other way. But it came about
That the ban to my surprise was lifted

Suddenly one fall
And I went to sea after all
And shaped a course away from the trees that framed the seascape
Beyond my mother's house, incandescent
Birches and fiery maples as well
As forbidding clouds of hemlock and pine, a forest that was
Like a terrestrial sky
But is much less so now in memory—I don't remember why. It
    was said
That a woman's presence on a ship at sea would bring disaster
    down
On every sailor aboard but the gods
Of mythology seem to have liked us well enough
Or maybe they liked us too well, chasing us in animal form
With violent winds. Then mythology gave
Way to history
And now history is going
The way of fairytales. A path, bricks, innocents—they are
    additions, but odd
Additions to oddity.
Gullibility is an expression of enthusiasm
So great it makes decisions. But I am throwing off conviction,
    bound
To regard the sea
As a prison holding people whom their childhood friends cannot
    believe
Capable of crime. It is midsummer and the sun is lost
In the sun, visibility is accomplished. Can credibility be far
Behind? I won't pretend
To be an historian, how could I, when I have no idea
Of today's date. Though I know we embarked one morning early
In May, I have no idea how long ago that was
And I don't care. I breathe, I twist my hair. I watch
The sea. At times it resembles an eye
But it isn't watching me. Some days ago a silent kayak
Appeared and then disappeared, winding through a lead

In the ice. The first mate kept close
Watch for several hours after the kayak, following a shimmering band of water
West, disappeared
Or, as the first mate put it, "withdrew"—the mate insisting
That the occupant might be a pirate
Outcast, enemy, spy
Or some other type with hostile intent
Emboldened by the ice
Approaching
In broad daylight. A strange expression. Soon there will be no more
Than a band of pink against the dark,
Narrow daylight
As at the beginning or end
Of a day in the habitable latitudes,
Where breadth is what is assumed of days
As it is of the sea even when mist closes in
Around the ship. She is called the *Distance* and we go where she goes and arrive
Willy-nilly at times and places of whose existence we'd known nothing before
And which therefore, though we come upon them inevitably, we reach
Involuntarily. There
Is always *somewhere* and always in or at it
Something—whether material or musical—
And it's to these that we hope to go and from these that we hope to return.
But beset by such hopefulness (cold,
Ominous, and calm) we're getting nowhere
And tempers are short.
I've grown hard of hearing, the first mate said sarcastically this morning,
Did you ask for a hard-boiled egg?
Jean-Pierre is no longer included in the games the other children

are playing—
Soon he'll be an adolescent, already he's hovering
Over the figurehead, a woman
Holding a telescope to her left eye.
For the most part it is trained on the horizon.
She is establishing herself.

II

How inviting circumstance can be!
All that's in view gives us the present. The world
We knew
Was always the same but the present
Is that
In which one can see everything
Differently, the waves as green lilies, the wind
As a bobbing water bird, the distance
As a concert hall, but our emotions
Are obscure. We need music. Hearing nothing
Is complicated. Play the lute. Play
The game. Bring lemons.
The planet seems young—raucous, ravenous, quick, and wet. The planet exists
With gusto. Things fall to it and sink, things are rooted in it
And rise. It's impossible
To clear the way and come within
Sight of my subject. Obscure
Emotions cling to it—obscuring emotions. The analytical imagination
Naturally undertakes analysis of the imagination
While the emotional imagination does what, emote? I've tried to give emotions
The slip
By attributing them to other people
Named Felix, Sasha, Nils, Miroire, and when a new one
Rises I will call it Sam
Or Angelique, an iffy strategy
At best. It's naïve to think their motives would correspond
To mine. Emotions get blown
Into beliefs
Attached to stories—explanatory traps for names. Jealousy,
Hope, worry, love seek out plots and find
Conditions, Nina, Hico, George-Allen, Rose. William fears

What he calls
Conditional ghosts
Which he says are near and live on the ice
More and more of which we've been seeing
Day and night passing us as we pass
If indeed we *are* passing. At times it seems as if we are simply riding
A swell back
And forth over a drop
Off into a trough at the edges of the barely habitable
World. A glance into the distance
Raises these doubts and I take shyness, pity, suspense
And pride as signs of aesthetic well-being
For which I can't account, the sea absorbs
Our inexplicable feelings. I suppose
We are drowning in saga.

III

Great cumulous clouds hang overhead
One moment and terns
Another. It is always safe
To predict variability. The light
On my face is cold and yet I often feel
Heat. Perhaps we are all small suns.
The sunflower in its pot on deck doesn't think
So. It turns
Frantically
But not to us
As the *Distance* rides the sea and sends the sun
Sliding
Violently into all the compass corners.
Am I compassionate? Or is it from some other species of
  enthusiasm
That I give a thumbs-up
As the *Distance* slows so as to pass
Gently through a flock of floating seabirds? Their kind must be
Persistent and have been here long
Before the first human flutterings
Whose persistence has brought us
Here to no end
Unless an anomaly can be termed an end.

IV

According to the Greeks metamorphoses have to be complete
And are impossible. Things may change
But nothing can become the opposite
Of what it is. The sky cannot
Be not the sky, the distance not distant. Yet
I can see it
Both ways. Then yet
Again I hardly remember who it was
I was instead of this
Back when I gazed
Up through branches tossing in the wind at the blue
Perimeters of the clouds and felt uprooted even
At an early age perhaps from gods, my deities
Were streaming
Or grinding like a boat being hauled over stony ground. The
    sound
Gives me pleasure still
Though it is fugitive. Pleasures are synonymous
With powers
And lest they become dangerous they *must* be
Fugitive. How strangely our course approaches
Forks, how variously we decide which tack
To take. We ourselves are fugitives,
The world is strange. It appears to last and appears so as to last
Through the dark of night or of storms into which it disappears
To last as well. We have come in
The dark upon landforms, shores, islands without knowing
What to expect. On some one may enter
Into friendship, on others into endless complaint.
But there must be more to friendship than a placid acceptance
Of misunderstandings and interruptions, though these have the
    effect
Of timely inevitabilities that we encounter
Constantly. Someone remarks "there's something

Over there" or, more urgently, "there's something ahead!"
The boat tacks —I say that though the engines are running.
We have no destination. One can't foretell
What may or may not be pointless. The boat
Arches, bends, turns—it is shaping itself. I dream
Confusedly that we've "varied" and come to an island
Which can be approached
Only through one of forty doors at each of which sits
A restlessly perched bird, some one of which may disclose some
singular logic
To me in an ancient seasonal language which I will understand.
The gist of what occurs according to the birds is repetitive
Unlikeliness (or unlikelihood—it isn't clear which). We are all so
busy
It seems sometimes that the only time we can appreciate
Existence is when we are at sea
Subject to capriciousness
Though we sleep slung in binding hammocks like spiders
Or netted fish or trapeze artists bouncing near
Ground level at the end of their act. At night
The several sequences of sea
Twist in turbulence. Observing the effects I grow vertiginously
Calm. How odd it is to be
Out. At best one can know only the knowledge
Of one's time. When one reaches
The limit of that one must make way
And I say so hospitably. Between ourselves
We speak the language of these parts. The communications are
never
Concise. Whatever we say is best understood
If contextualized, so contexts are
What we say, and they too are best understood if contextualized
And so it goes, sometimes inward and sometimes outward
Bound not round
And round but as if over the bridge
From top to toe

Or pegbox to tailpiece
Of a vast violin strung
To what we think of as strung
And we cling to it as to a shroud.

V

William insists that his ghosts are disenchantments
And they're watching
Him, he wants more wind, more speed, and more sea
Life to appear, he believes the bright herring
And blue terns keep the ghosts at bay. He says all of us
Have them—doppelgangers, biographers,
And matchmakers—they are the shadows
Of our knowledge returning echoes
From events. It's the life in them
That does this, William says, and Miroire concurs.
Life is likely
To be haunting
And it's haunted, too, the mysterious whales
Possessed by life blow
And a glaucous gull even now
Sits in its body on the railing and stares
Out to sea where the real thing
About real things is that they are spooky. I'm often afraid
But never reluctant, though I find the job of cataloguing
The intellectual passions difficult and as for describing them—
Forget it. It's probably just some trace
Of anxiety disguised as fervor that makes me judge
The effort worthwhile, the voyage good.
It seems as if my certainty
That my fears are justified
Has not only contributed to my amazement, my sustained sense
Of being surprised
By myself, alive
And not only that but here,
It has also engendered relief
Of the kind one feels when, through some act of generosity
And comprehension, justice is done—justice
Not vengeance, which is a very different thing. I cannot help but rail

Even now, so many weeks after
We set sail past the prison
In which only three nights later a man was to be put
To death. Meticulous pseudo-medical preparations and sadistic
  scene-setting
Were underway as we went by, part
Of a prolonged vicious ritual. It used to be
That people fled to these latitudes to escape
Such barbarity. The man—whoever he was—must be dead now.

VI

Sharp as sleet, they say, this over
Sweeping. It's nostalgia (or Miroire's
Grief) with which we're hit
With the gist of history
From which memories are cut off
Like the realms of Lear from Lear or the little match girl's
Proper heat lost in mist
Moving in cold caught in a curve
No more than an inch
From the flame that leaps and fails
To shrink it. Mirages loom in the air
That is the whole horizon and not
At liberty. There is nothing
Melancholy about them. The distance between us
Provides them with a stage
On which an elaborate prank is underway
Far from land and free
To come out now that there is nothing
To get in the way. At first
Greta insisted that she could hear the bleating of a kitten or
    perhaps a howling
Goat or lamb, I heard it
Too, and she climbed some distance up the rigging
To get the better view
That the distance can provide
Only to witness the entire scene
Dissolve like white sugar in clear water
Into nothing when she was precisely 14 feet above deck
And though it materialized—but vague
And wrong as the opinions the outside world has of one's
    mother—
When she was down again, the kitten, goat, or lamb had fallen
Silent, which proves to me that a mirage can make itself
Audible or not. Often

Even when we don't know where we are
We think we know what's around us, but what's around us
Is where we are and if the latter
Which we term
There consists of floating particles
Then the former
Which we call
Here is likely to do so too
Emitting noise and scattering colors—mauve, gray-green, and
  russet
For the credulous—at least briefly. Yes, said Greta: briefly. Then
  Nathan
Hauled the dripping net of sharpened laundry on deck
And we gathered round to shake, soften, sort, and hang our
  things,
Collective things since the clothing no longer has individuality
And perhaps we have lost ours, too. Matching sock to sock
Took up an hour
And by then the mirages had all dissolved and the bleating
Creature (whatever it was) had drowned.
We went below for supper (beans
Again, a wedge of lemon, and herring on bread).

VII

A sense of well-being, excitement, and resignation—all of these
At once but separately in a single sense—
Comes over me now
And then unsummoned and unwarranted in this time-within-time
By which we are surrounded. I note, sketch, and chart
With results that seem both
As private as conversation and as public
As the scientific record. My shipmates—companions—and I are
intimate
But like islands, isolated
So as to escape
Interference. And now "and now"—eventfulness abounds
But there is no news. We share a common edifice, condition, time
And are equally and (within the confines
Of our small universe) universally
Informed. Such understanding as we have we generate
Together and together gain. Maybe
This doesn't make a world
But it has made for something like a convexity
Of consciousness. We can't put everything into it. "A toy, a wind-
mill...
To make it whirl the faster." "Gulp!" We search
Emotion, memory, abstract
Thought, even hallucination
And dream
For news
And no doubt
Like the others as I've trembled in the cold
I've searched the cramped interstices between my body's tremors
For peaches, communicable insights, reading lists, anecdotes.
The body must be the register
Of place—in the minute
And uncontrollable quick shivering and shifting postures
Something about the substance

Of time may be shown. Perhaps
It is. I thrill fearfully to the encyclopedic
Passions. Study
Emphasizes the paths to form
Rather than the form itself, they say,
But from forms I find myself looking back
In search of paths
Out again. You would think
One might appear when I sneeze,
Sneezing being the work of the gods, or so I've read,
Since one can neither will it into existence nor prevent it
When it occurs, but consider the sequence
Of scenes we've beheld, the series
Of islands we've encountered and events
We've experienced—they can't be taken together
To represent anything, not even the stretch
However long—I've lost track as I've said
Of time. At various hours I've mounted my camera
On the railing of the *Distance,* one day
I had Samuel take it to the crow's nest
And I left it taking shots 30 minutes apart
For 24 hours of the face of an iceberg
To windward as we sheltered beside it. Images
All lead the eye to places
Flatter than they should be. Too flat. One has got to be quicker.
Trust peripheral vision, peripheral consciousness,
Even peripheral conscience—is it some cultural residue
That makes me feel so bad? The sea sorts plumes, then throws them
To the wind
Without inhibition.
We anchor to map water
To which we're anchored
In salt. Is it the salt
That brings down spirals?
Long ago was fated to find us. Everything adds up. Can we
    contribute?

VIII

Wing-wing with playful perversity
Says numbers as the Romans do, on my birthday
I'll be x
She says, but we are not in Rome, still
She repeats, the Captain says we haven't touched land
In cliv days, and Madoud's amused. Cliv today, he says,
And clv tomorrow
As if wittily or winningly
Stripping twigs
From timbers for a hull or fuel. Wing-wing's prattle is like pig
Latin—easier for her to say than for us
To understand. We can't begin
A new life in these circumstances. There's no proof
That we are here or that we aren't.
Madoud's mathematical calculations are written
As if in salt, we converse as if over stolen cell phones. It's not
  quick
Thinking that will save us. The constant commentary of the sea is
  so slow
The simplest remark can take it years
To utter. Its beauty is rational, sure, but we'll never get to the end
Of its reasons. We've only words for wind, reduced. Dim
I figure, did mix mid lid mid vim did vid dix did
To ten. We'll never come to the end
Of our poisons—so Pascal says.

IX

Pathos has sea legs, Pathos
Is a white monkey of a dog
Appointed Pathos
And nautical. Pathos
Leaps into the shrouds
Of the *Distance* and watches
Game for play
Into which she'll plunge
Eager as a soul
For Pathos feels
That nothing exists
In which Pathos isn't meant
To share, little masochist, as Miroire says.

X

The verdict is that we're assailed. Perhaps
By ambivalence. Unerringly it tracks us. My own wavering
Comes up like the forceful dawn
And pulls me after what will follow
With new logic that's just reaching
Into vague places—logic that tries
Both laughable and admirable
Apparitions, a daylight practice, rules
To come
That never get any closer than purple is to green. There's always
something
In between—not some front
Line of defense (like Pathos yapping at Regret)
But choices still and still
To be made just
As noises are made by Abby
And Feliz—they're the noisiest of us and their knowledge remains
Disorganized. But wars do pertain
To foresight and disbelief
To ambivalence. So I'm back
And beginning
Freely—I confess to it. Jane insists
That I take ambivalence as a virtue, not a flaw. Why not
Rescue beginning from scorn, she says,
Just as one would rescue someone afloat
Drifting on a raft. One would, of course—across any space
whatsoever—
But there's no reason to suppose
That one will like what one has saved.
I say so somewhat maliciously, thinking of the hateful
Regret rescued from a log somewhere
Off Tierra del Fuego three years ago and now
Confined to a stinking cage
Which she (Jane thinks she's female) filthies (she even shits

In her water dish) and into which I stare
Without being able to discover any grounds at all
For affinity. I should settle for parallelism.
But a writer of annals, chronicles, journals, diaries,
Or history
Ventures to discover affinities
As a cartographer ventures to discover a place. I look at the cage
From different points of view, the creature looks
As it did before, so I begin
With that in mind: mortal and finite. The sooner
The better, William says, and though I don't say so
I think the same and start. But we are stuck
With Regret—when the ship struck
The sinking log on which she was adrift and Jane
And the Captain pulled her aboard, they struck an obligation
With her
And it involves us all—as long as she lives
She will die, and within
Those terms (these being the outer limits
Of her existence, neither of which she can cross, since birth
Severed her irreversibly and eternally
From the state of never-having-existed and death
Would sever her from living) her life
Spans an eternity and for the duration of that
Eternity (for her eternity) she is
From log to cage, from the southern ocean to the northern seas,
The selfsame creature: reptilian and green, and that
She is that
Is no less wondrous than Jean-Pierre's
Being Jean-Pierre from one hour to the next
Though he is sure from one moment to the next that each
moment is
Freeing him from the previous one and releasing him
To the next—a real moment for the real
Jean-Pierre. I remember
Patches of my own adolescence as I catch glimpses

Of patches of turbulence the wind is picking up, tearing
At the surface of the sea
But in those days my imagination drew thick forests
Into which I would dash
Into a secret future
Between trees, walking the forest floor on the outer edges of my
feet —
Silent, invisible, in an infinite process of disappearing.

XI

We are used to being reviled as makers of metaphors
And feared. Men have accused us
Of witchery, they've accused us of receiving
Visitations and crafting
Transmutations; we are blamed
For changes, the more precise the more terrifying. But fate is
Down everyone's alley, in everyone's line,
Though fulfilling it is involuntary,
It follows
What follows. They say that
An ability to recognize one's fate
Constitutes wisdom since vanity
In following is impossible—impossible
To indulge. On the other hand, the more following is foiled
The more irritated we become. For weeks on end the winds
whipped us
Around and now the calm leaves us to hang. Whited-out, I
despair
Of getting myself right and if that's not the despair
Of the vain I don't know what is.
Humorlessly the humorless cook has been trying
To force me into explanations. I communicate
Nothing. It could be I'm lazy,
But no one has said as much. I have a stack of pages to my credit,
after all.
I've drawn elevations, projected horizons, balanced rocks
On waves, and I can declare that in both there is as much past as
future. But what
Of the present? I'm projecting horizons I can't see. I might as well
be writing
Novels, it being the point of fiction as of science to enable us to
perceive
How others live, how other things are.
They exist like us, alone.

XII

Bit by bit the horizon lowers
Like a limbo stick
And back
Inch by inch we bend
Leaning more
And more like lovers low
To duck
The bar, the ban, the barrier, the war
Or fall. Is that
It? The ship's
Inevitable dip
Of which we're never rid and always fight
To ride
In our willful life
Back
To back with the things in life we do not will
And reel
With the sounds in the sounds
Like fish
And wake behind the ship. Does it fit?

XIII

A chronicler must gather details as if they were hard candies
That will be given (though only later) to people
Who will put them in their mouth to suck
With fascination for a long time.
But what grey mountains of water they are in reality
Lifted by sand and then toppled
Into foam
That strikes at us. We cannot gulp it down. It scuds
And like an aggregate of prisms
Studies the light
By which we see (or think we see) where we are, what's there, past sinking into
Our wake and future on the horizon
Or on one of the several horizons
That float
In bands
Or present objects distorted but still recognizable
As they might be to a time traveler
Between the vanishing line and the limiting line
Streaking the sky
With islands
Of enormous but non-existent beauty
Offering us nothing but unproductive gladness.

XIV

We are on one side of memory, this side. But this means that
Only half of death is wasted
On us. Of the other half we know nothing. We will be taken
One by one. By pelicans. By
Fists. We'll flail, resist
With what's called living
As we must, dying. Each horizon calls up others
And if they are obscure to the apathetic
It's because the apathetic make poor judges: they lay down
Their spheres.
It's been said that nature never makes a jump
But that's inaccurate. Accuracies are disparate
And variously horizoned. Things pitch
Through the orders of event, they drop
Into the turning of the line through the dark
To every day from top to bottom
Or so I hear from a rising internal voice
That is now dying away. I'd recommend that you check
The map, it was saying—once you drown
You remain drowned
And what the left eye saw and the right eye interpreted
As "before" will be one
With what the right eye saw and interpreted
As the "outcome"
For which we didn't volunteer. But I've done a lot
Of volunteering, I'd respond. I'm willful
And I'm here (specifically)
As a result, sometimes fustrated, frenzied (capture and freedom
Are the same) but like the dead, still on deck, dead
But not offstage. Half-obscured
By fog my father appeared some days ago, he had his paints.
Mortality can be traced—it is
Vivid—cerulean, ochre, veridian
And black. I move to see,

Montage to understand, I pass the camera
To others so as to emancipate the point of view. Trade is relevant
Everywhere. We can't escape economy, economies.
As far as we can see the world
Is unsparing of things to see, reality
Is profligate, ubiquitous, vivid, prolix, it's all too much, vista
Without terrain, *the* "too much," the "neither given nor giveable"
World we can neither approach nor leave. We live
Then through. Then having lived, we will always have
Lived. The only immortality is absence.

XV

Subjectless we come
Up like birds on a wall, the shadow
Of an opening door swinging over a man, looking
Down—it must have been a fear of depths, not heights—
   freedom's best
Images are horizontal ones—the fun
Of racing horses, fanning radio waves, a jigsaw puzzle, slabs
Of bread, rhyme and consequence quivering, lag time,
   surreptitious
Extensions across the floorboards—and up—into walls of the sun
As if half-surprised that the world is there at all. My bedroom was
   papered
In a non-deciduous green, bed set like doubt, head against
The wall between two windows looking back toward a clock
   tower, four-faced
And forgiving, as far as I remember—wind, moon sliding
Past clouds, rebellious vows—but rebellion is a bad alternative,
   they say
To revolution. Back through incidents, perceptions, we search
Through a series of hesitations among anomalies
No more anomalous than we
For reality—how
Do we know, how did we learn, to do this?
Wherein lies our capacity for uncharacteristic perceptions,
   inexplicable
Ideas, impressions of humans, say, so huge
They could wade across the sea
Making it seem shallow, and ahead
Through emptiness for thoughts
Like arctic boaters through melting leads. We set forth of our own
   volition
And—lose control of our course through no fault
Except perhaps that of our course with its pulse:
Engine, anthem, ease, a gale. There's a saga! Samuel

Has been telling Miroire of the time
Traveler after a disaster sent back into the past to change
The conditions that will bring the disaster to pass. It's of a task
Whose success requires the time traveler to remember the future
Rather than the past. Pascal will not let the paradox escape
Him. "It is said that those with a bad memory
Have bad memories," he says. We come upon
Evocative (some might even say animate) debris, evidence
Of no particular situation, no particular person's history
Or character—it's the absolutely uncharacteristic that freaks us out. Pathos
Barks, the Captain sneezes. We are given things
To remember—a pyramid of oranges, a bloodied pond—but we go
Get some, too, "setting forth on what promises to be
A memorable adventure," etc., and we're advised
To take layers. Pathos might more aptly have been called
Prattle. Where the colors driven by the wind
Apply, history returns, and so can I, having told myself these things
And keeping them in readiness to tell again.

XVI

Courage—that takes time, haste and exhaustion
Produce cowards. Heroes whether villainous, fat, towering, fair
Game for ridicule, or feminine as animals
In sagas must row into their stories
Like children
Chasing a ball, shoes flying from their feet like wings
Of petrels
Whose stormy flight
From war might bring us home if there were wind to accompany
The fife-and-drumming of the wind
That permeates our thoughts just as experience
Permeates events and makes us wonder
Why we came. These are no one else's days
But they're not quite ours so are we brave? The *Distance* has endless hours rarely
Interrupted except by an occasional egg and the celebratory clucking in the wake
Of its laying by a grey hen or a white one while we boldly long
For something red or yellow as the forgotten sun. Nothing burns
As cruelly as the cold and we have nothing
To burn but that—well
That and the *Distance* whose hold holds
Onions still and lemons hard
As coal, their slippery seeds
The bumps
On their rind, their tips
Their ends
And entire singular selves
Maintaining the continuous record of a curve. Go.
Go, store, soul, and soul, go, know.

XVII

Even in my dreams I'm shocked
By the criminality that dreams permit. Awake
I'm too much the quaking coward for crime. I confess.
Remorse comes readily to me. And yet
I don't tend to look back—that's not my cast of mind—I imagine
Life launched and landed, in waiting as at hand, pitch
And obsidian and plains. But recently when squeezed
In the constraints of a free bunk—
Not 'mine'—not anyone's—we sleep like animals in transit—
And unnecessarily watchful I walk
Imaginary walks
Through places I thought I'd never see again
As they were when I was a child
Since they no longer exist
Except in and to—prepositions are the boldest terms—a mind
Set back. Of course.
The objects of retrospection are absent, one can't do anything
About the past. But reality is never anonymous, it's permeated
With personality plunged into particulars which in their turn
    compose it and seeing that
Is a philosophical act. Only thinking
Can survey the task
And so it goes,
I'm in a bunk
With hardly room to turn
From left side to right, and I like to do that,
Turn from side to side and then, sometime later, turn again
To renew sleep and all that it promises
Secretly. The pleasure is intense, reduced
To an adventure
Lasting only an instant
But that instant begins the hour, the experience, the dream
Of a perspicacious owl with a cruel beak
Emerging from a package bound in red paper

To sigh
As an infant does just before it wakes
Sucking its gums as if nursing at a milky current of thought.
Its flow is slow
But it can never be drained, there's never any end
To it. The luminosity of the fog
Defies all attempts to describe it. There's nothing yellow, nothing jaundiced
To the light,
The sun is blue,
It must be,
And a moth is fluttering over the logbook, its shadow
At these latitudes
Seems miniscule
And that insignificance at these latitudes seems momentous. Over the logbook
Jean-Pierre may be thinking something similar. Scale!
Scale!
I said to him this afternoon. And I could see that he was trying to think
Of something funny
To say in response
But in the end all he could come up with was a comment—
'The world cannot love us'—
And I laughed
At him and his bit of lugubrious, rebellious bathos,
While altogether I missed
That he'd said 'us' and that included
Nils, who has just whimpered in his sleep
And Nina, who has whispered
Hush, and me.

XVIII

Turbulence is about, like time, there is nothing
Beyond
The symbolic disorder that stirs
Oceanic feelings in the dismal projections that cast
Boats into storms like parodies of the buoyant
Imagination. Madoud says that the gods can suddenly grant a
    wave
Astonishing beauty
But the change is imperceptible to humans. So is the turbulence
That the gods, were there any, would leave
In their wake (and there would be nothing but wake
Were there gods)
Or ghosts
Given to the syntax of the sea
So far as these words now are
From war and here in "sultry August dusk
Time than death dumber." Frozen
Out, the distance frozen in
Not time-congealed labor
But trauma-congealed time
Presses against the distance
With the force of music—loud with drums—nothing
Interrupts us—we are *in* an interruption: boats
Into storms
Imperceptible to the humming shrouds
In pairs that guy the mast
In mist
Or glaring glossy clarity
Which is perfect and perfectly refuses
Dialectic. Big word, says Miroire, coming on deck. Call me
He says
The opposite—
Of what?—
Of clarity hardly

Known
Of storm
We hardly know
Not knowing storm
For which we yearn with wind
That will straighten us out who are limp
As sails or casual friends or innocuous colleagues with mediocre
 ambitions
And reluctance to cause a flap, ha-ha, I'll go
On deck
Once more.

XIX

The woman who sets sail will cross
Reefs, science is the practice of unknowing, and given
Enough time every circumstance will betray
What it promised
To guarantee—these
Are, as I've discovered, inconclusive, uninhibited
Observations—all as allegorical
As the rooster's "cock-a-doodle-do"
Which I can accurately quote but in no way understand.
All in all
There is very little containment in the universe
Except what's temporarily contained in the bodies
Of things as presence
Or in animate bodies as life. The sea
Is never silent—it subjects one to sound—that's the only name I know
For the distance. It has noisy spans.
They *rumble* and *splash* as the ropes *pong*
Against the stanchions, the decks *roar*
With cold. I know these words.
My thoughts are dead without them.

XX

Feliz is setting dominoes on track with Jane
As company reading
Nina's book to Nils. Dusk can get no darker. Diminuendo
Is set to reverse. Miroire's admiring the noise
Verbs, which he's adding to his English next to rice
And radish, rhyme and cold. The ice
He says is still but never quiet. It sings,
It crackles, pings. It groans
Like land as it falls away
As cows vast as tractors buoyant as balloons do
Stumbling downhill through mud at dusk
In heartfelt anticipation of hay
Flung from bails bound like bricks and stacked
Like commemorative volumes of Longfellow's verse
Near a wall sheltering a hutch of girlish rabbits. We have only two
Left. William has his lines out
To save them but their very smell hovers
Like earthy inevitability lurking
Decidedly. That's what it means then to be
Out of place. And what would it mean to be out
Of distance
Like a foal, an onyx young animal, translucent as memory
When one seeks to remember
Some person, place, moment, or thing and bring
It close enough to see? Everywhere lack of distance
Introduces supposition, crush, and verticality
Prevails like an instant inadvisably left in a knot, ship
Above ship below. Memory, circulating, dips. The sea
Is dark, sea gray. The sea
Is slow. Sea following sea flat
Far from the horizonless sea war.

XXI

William's ghosts are paranoid thoughts: no!
They are protests against the confusion
Of universal and particular. William is an advocate
Of argument. But I'm too timid
For the words that come
To mind, they've badly miscalculated when they present
Themselves to me.

XXII

The *Distance* has the power of a body
Which is the power of death
And we are captives of it, busily at work,
Because we love life. Yet in the end
That life—boundless and immeasurably strong
And which we feel so strongly
To have taken form for us
As our own individual life —
Cannot protect us from the sea
Anymore than I can imagine a triangular gray
Or believe that it is merely a wire fence that keeps the dead
grandfather
From appearing out of the distance
In his little boat, camera in hand,
Or the dead aunt in her khaki uniform after one long war
And a little before another, starched, shod, and prepared
For a drive through the countryside that she said reminded her of
champagne
Which she pronounced
And I heard as sham pine
Proving what I already knew, that she was a mock soldier and a
real fool.
I took things literally; I equated the literal with the authentic.
And I expected
More of women than of men back then.
Willa Cather never disappointed me. Nor did my mother's
mother
Who took me with her to take photographs of oaks
Through a lens veiled in cheesecloth
And once we were away from home and on the forest road
She'd put the jeep in first gear and let me steer
Over rough terrain bouncing like a motorboat
On a rough sea, flight shattered and yet remaining flight,
The passenger bound to the unbinding of the world's surface

From the world. As a child there was nothing I liked better
Than chocolate pudding with its skin
Which was always darker than what lay beneath it. I skimmed
It gently and scientifically off.
It clung to the spoon.
I sucked at it.
And once it was gone I drew patterns in the soft, vulnerable
    pudding, excising
And eating as I drew
All the way down to the bottom of the sea.

XXIII

Drawn by desire, our own, as if autobiographically, we go
On intensions
Intentionally without intentions we can know
Undertaking aimless motion
Or motion for its own sake
Pursuing a vibration that we take for a grebe
But that seems next to have been
No more than a spasm
Of the eye which sees almost unconsciously
The flickering at the edge
To which, holding a camera, I've held
My breath. The glare
Is not for signaling. But what if preferring to hold
Desire intending something I lack, I lack
The will to carry it out? I want to understand
What I have seen and understand
That nothing I have seen explains what I have seen.
Like that.

XXIV

We have a concept of justice
Despite the fact that asymmetry is ubiquitous
And constantly throws things off-balance. But then
We are a tilted species
Dipping and lunging forward, swinging our baskets
Of eggs, stuck to our shadows
Which gravity in turn sticks to life
Throughout the long days that night disarrays.
The fog is taking shape, it is forming
Gulls and longshoremen, dolphins and cities
It sweeps from a sliding circle
Whose circumference lies beyond the edges of the field
Of vision by which we are engulfed. It leaps
From under a sheet and mumbles a sound that might have been a
word—
It was probably not. It is late
Afternoon before it hesitates. It says something
Inseparable from what it doesn't say
But of course that would be the case—we're talking about music.
A buzzer goes off.
Dawn is drawn.
And this is a dawn advancing impressions
At sea. Advance. The excitement curls up
As if around a pin or a lost stick,
Walking and otherwise. But one can't reserve it
Anymore than one can reserve one's place at sea
Though we've selected the sea
As have the clouds. The shadows of the clouds fall
On the *Distance*
Which they stick to the sea.

XXV

The distance lies low on the horizon and placid
As a sheep that's lain down exhausted
By its very plumpness
Which is half the secret of its visibility, the other
Being light. Time
Will tell, but I think I'll never be
Happy with my memory of it. Ocean
As dusk, dusk as a sunken sandbar, and we ourselves milky
As infants, impotent, incomprehensible, dependent
On everything, sure
To remember nothing, the rigging
Humming for no reason like a woman in a kitchen, the sound
Of an empty, nonexistent bell ringing
In the air, and no one is alarmed, asleep
Or busy. It's the force of meaning
That will take us into the distance
Bound somewhere to a shore—memorable
Insects, dust, moss, frogs. Forgetfulness is as impermanent as a
    holiday
Party where all the drinks are sweet, a bit of glossy candy clings
To the hostess's lower lip, and a faint line of salt
Lies on a baby's cheek left behind by its tears, its sex
Indiscernible as it sleeps
In its yellow shirt away from the hubbub, the creaking
And the music coming into the foreground that someone is just
    turning up,
An overture of some sort promising consequence but it's only
    music
That like the time-traveling hero sent to repair the past
Can remember the future. Human groups in isolation
Develop dialects. Nina has heard egrets
As regrets and everyone's taken to calling them
That. We've left them behind.

XXVI

Fog, abstractions, nothing
To see. What then to think of? Thought itself. Quietly. Time's
  worth
The wait. Feliz, Wing-wing, and Abby pass
An hour or two in planning. I remember how pleasant it is
To plan
But also how pernicious it is always to foresee
Plans fail. We're foiled before
We're troubled, we've sailed
As if into a photograph
Along a continuous curve
Taken by a war
Correspondent. There is no resolution, only cruel thought
Through thickening obscurity that turns
To mock the monologuing mind. A person can't lie
Without being aware of it. Snow falls, fills
The metal bucket burying a rope
That Clara coiled inside it like a snake
In the ice obscured by our exacerbated attention to motives,
  freezing
Motifs. A new mirage has appeared, a shopping mall, or country
Fair, all the performers are seeking approbation. Time is the
  continuation
Of existence, they say. We catch the moment
Of a wall's collapse, we see a snowball
Fight, then a train puffing steam pulls into a station, children
  jump
Off a jetty thrown into the sea, all pattern
Broken, as if in the aftermath of the last sea-battle
After which there would be no sea-battling again.

XXVII

Time leans, then speeds. It brings wind. We run
Wishfully. Necessity unkindly plunges. I love
Yet reality is in thrall to imagination
And love is drained by cowardice.
Things come out of infinity—appearance—a fog—
And they are differentiated into opposites at war
With one another. The victory of any results
In injustice to the rest. And then atonement must be made
By the victor. The fog must atone, then the wind, then the *Distance,* then the sea
In which the island we've sighted seems to stand alone,
Hiding its mysteries as if it were a strip of over-exposed film
Or a darkening chrysalid hanging like a question,
Serene, even bovine, covered
With flowers that like us are capable of imagining
Themselves. It is said that a person in love is impatient
And for what? For love: categories get filled with examples.
Heights, depths—who knows what they may be? I can tell you everything
That we know about rats but I can't tell you what rats know
About themselves. We brought two flop-eared rabbits with us, both
Gray, we thought them bucks
But then there were ten. Now two again, they rest
With hind legs extended. If they could only bring horses
To mind that would be a consolation. But peaceful years appear in history only
As interludes, pauses lacking content, their history
Driven out of them
When the despot is overthrown
And the power has yet to go
To those who even now as we sail on are inventing the conflict
Which they will seize. History
Will record this. Anticipation of it is already elegiac.

But freedom is not dependent on time nor on money. Freedom is dependent
On nothing.

XXVIII

Pathos is in for what Feliz calls
A plump dunking—play
The children—little Brechtians—have underway
And not just for Pathos but for all of us. Nils says that
It will be a saga and that it will pass the time. If you're in
A play you have to remember lines, Abby
Says, you have to remember not to forget them
Too, says Nina. Jean-Pierre lifts Pathos like a child
To dandle high and low. Acting is muscular.

XXIX

It's true I cannot see my face
Because it's always facing. I cannot see my thoughts
Because they're always thinking, fading in
And out of absent things, comprised of pointless motions
That push me ahead of myself
With worry, curiosity
Unposed, unformed, unframed. Continuous
With what accompanies them, dark,
Light
Lighting the never elemental elements
And surrounding surface fabric phantoms
That make up the so-called apparent life about which we think
We've nothing true to learn. Thinking takes to the distance, speeds
To outrace what we'll never learn
And so we have to go on and on into the following
Day which we are so much accustomed to think of
As a long (but not too long) new day
Bringing with it the potential for remedy
Should remedy be needed
For whatever happened yesterday (which in any case has slipped
Away and lies over us now
As stupid as the sand
Hiding a flounder
Because the flounder has swirled it off the sea bottom and let it drift
Over itself) that we tend to regard actions
As free
Defining them as that which can't be saved
While we clutch at the newness of the supposedly new day
Not to deny, accept, ameliorate, or modify events
But to eliminate remorse. But nothing is free,
We are passing through cascades of animation
And even that which is 'merely imaginary'
And that which is overlooked
Soak us.

XXX

We are surrounded by immobilized projections.
The sails slat and the rigging drips
Into a reflecting sea. We can easily forget
Whether it is night or day that is thrust forward
Whether we are awake or asleep. Our mappings are as arbitrary
As words—they are mere estimates, juttings, externalizations.
Experts say that the emotions begin
And end in the body
Equally inescapable and capable of escape
But like Mercator we have cast them
With straight meridians and arcing parallels
Though the results chime inconclusively with what we see.
Good bones and waves and weights all slide into the status of
  reasons
And slip away again. Only the *Distance*
Blinded by the fog hardly dares to move. Decisions draw
A blank. Sasha is pale. I feel calm.
Detached.
Frozen.
Hardly alive.
But that's normal, no cause for alarm
Which I wouldn't sound even if I could. I am here.
Hardily alive, then
Alive, hard at it,
That is. Yes.
The stanchions are humming. I put my hand on the shrouds, face
Forward, and hear
Radio signals, a voice, then
Music, now speaking
"The episode herself," "a rise
In worker output rolling"
"Per hour the rule"
"Unsung"—
Drifting imprecisely.

XXXI

We've left! We've arrived! The sentimental *Distance*
Parts the sea
With irony
Which is all that separates our arrivals from our departures
And the one who was Patrick from the one he is
Now—a soldier named Pascal fleeing war. He calls
The hens pecking for vermin on deck
"Stomping crevice mares"
And at night, unable to sleep, he counts with pen
Or as he puts it "threes":

don't paddle back
all curious delegates
I'll send puns

Mumbling four nights ago
Delighted by deception:

sleep o sleep
don't come yet
but come now

I'm still at sea, said Patrick/Pascal this morning:

float wobbled ducks
on deep dropping acreage
and peck at it

The birds always come early or they come late
As Clara from the cloud forms reads
Constantly
To the Captain
In his sleep. A false dog satisfies. A bird
Is a stroke of fate. That's

The difference
Doing something just
As it happens. A litter
Of pigs in a November romance
Is a free reality. In every woman's autobiography
Each and every thing at a time touches
The face of someone herself at a distance
Not yet done
With what she knows
She's done. The emotions
Hang things together
And when it comes to them one must rule
And be over-ruled
Loosely. Life can't be studied
As if it were the nonlife of something
Lived by someone studying. Isn't all autobiography
About which I'm disposed to be uncertain
About how things can't cohere
Sentimental? Doubt grasps
At the very thing
It doubts. Silence is the name for it
Clearly perceived
As the day fades
And its fading pales further. The first element
To impose its influence on me was my life. But life cannot stem
The onslaught
Of meaningfulness. I've committed
That to paper, 'that of which one cannot speak,' 'I'
Registering a boundary. That's sentimental
Which is what all ruptures generate
And all gaps demarcate
And there's no 'and so' nor 'but' nor 'meanwhile'
That can limit the irony. Irony *is* the limit.

XXXII

Every traveler's tale unfolds
Along the rising and falling contours
And over the edges
Written around the map
Of the tale folded into it. We are exposed. There is nothing here
But exposure. Every wave, even as it curls over the light, produces
 exposure,
Every thought is crossed by its own frame of illimitable
Transient foam. Exposure produces the blanks on the map
Which are as blindingly bright as the white light that the sun casts
Through the translucent mist
And that is the source of vision. The sun
Is always prejudiced in favor of appearances—change,
 eventfulness
And destination. One cannot die invisibly
In its presence.

XXXIII

The sea is inert, as if cautious
Or does it lurk? It holds
Back, it is ominous
And persuasive, yes, we are
Persuaded—at the source
Of our suspense, the sea
Is like the kayak to which the Captain everyday refers
Anxiously on the horizon which is perhaps the horizon
Itself penetrating to this effect and giving us something
To stare at
At a distance. I'm sorry, Carlotta said
An hour ago to Jane. No one can envy Carlotta, Carlotta cannot
envy
Jane. All our speculative murmurs
Malicious as the stink of Regret's cage or a dying rat
Somewhere behind the boards regarding Carlotta's incapacity
For empathy were wrong. Jane had badly barked
Her shin, cutting back a thick flap of skin to lay
Bare the bone that slid…
Ay: volunteer…like a fish past
A ship…word
Within…it was nothing
That the Engineer with his storm-blue thread couldn't fix. Now
Jane flags
And the *Distance* follows
Like a game that's afoot
And bound over blue
And buff slabs the worn color of boots
On land if land
It is that William pictures when he dreams
Of dropping lines.

XXXIV

There's only an inside to an emotion, there's nothing
On it to grasp, nothing
To be seen of it, it's nothing
But a structure without a form, a structure incapable of producing
A form, I feel all that I feel but there's nothing
There, nothing
Could be there: an emotion is held
In an absence together only
With the strength of an interior—anterior—presence.
But happily the world has poles
And they draw things out
Just as night draws
Bats from barns —I remember them from bed
When I was awake at dawn
And drawn myself
As if from soot
Without artistry or expertise
As green and purple, red and blue, yellow and green, all murky in
the end
But of course "end"
Isn't what waking
Entails
And self-
Portraiture is disdained
By scientists be they cartographers, physicists,
Or ichthyologists speeding briefly
On hard soil grasping at air.

XXXV

Jean-Pierre announces. Freedom is on stage. Pascal bows
Who was Patrick. History flows through verbs and is divided
Into tenses. I am she, he says. We can compare it
To love. When the actors look out
Over the audience at a ship just coming into view
The audience becomes an ocean, its members sailors. We drop
The sails, cut the engine, and let the boat drift
To show that we have not left the world, we are being taken by it.
True—our adaptation to land
Life is defunct and the things we say line up and wait
To take their turn in a series of little flights
And then they separate. Pathos barks. A girl changes herself
Into a spider and another spits out her tongue. The *Distance* rolls.

XXXVI

Lengthily the panic of an afternoon reverie speeds across
My wake. I was—like Jean-Pierre or Jane, even
Nils, Miroire, sailors and sympathizers, historians
And engineers with names—imagining
Myself as I might be
Imagined.
It is just such a symbolic involution, just such
A manifestation of the unsightly remains
Marking every intersection
That marks us for mortality. We are beset
Between closing longitudes
To the north of a small island
We have named 'The Lesser Null,' Madoud's
Idea. An occasional breeze
Comes up, but the *Distance* resists it
Just as a joke resists explication. Still
The children are less playful and the adults
Less certain. Letter-writing has broken out
Addressed to a person or persons sitting not ten feet away
Producing documents that are long and distant
As if composed with the caution of the shipwrecked. Now it will
    be our job
To exercise genius and associate words
Freely, with the adventurer's female abandon and the
    shipwrecked's
Resourcefulness, and it is neither memory nor clairvoyance
But simultaneity that is needed
For this, a challenge
That proves a metaphysical principle, though no one can know
To what it might apply. The northern waters are as black as ink,
The southern waters are pale in contrast—but the contrast itself is
    nowhere
To be found. When a complete metamorphosis occurs, the
    onlooker may marvel

But the metamorphosed cannot. Carlotta has asked
If I think we have souls and if they know we have bodies too. But why
Not ask, said Jean-Pierre, if we have bodies and if they know
We have souls? The historical naïveté of adolescents
Should be bracketed; it makes little sense
Except in its own position.

XXXVII

We have no Prospero to wreck us
And turn us into mules with dazzling haunches
Or geese in a saga sung to lyres
Around a fire blazing over buried treasure
On land we don't remember coming to.
The future has acquired the habit of waiting to reveal itself.
History should come next, as if it were a wind
That could make us happy.

About the Author

Lyn Hejinian is a poet, essayist, and translator. Her groundbreaking book of poetry, *My Life,* published by Green Integer, has had five re-printings since 1980. Her most recent books include *A Border Comedy* (Granary Books, 2001), *Slowly,* and *The Beginner* (both published by Tuumba Press, 2002), and *The Fatalist* (Omnidawn, 2003). The University of California Press published a collection of her essays entitled *The Language of Inquiry* in 2000. Translations of her work have been published in Denmark, France, Spain, Japan, Italy, Russia, Sweden, China, Serbia, and Finland. Since 1976 Hejinian has been the editor of Tuumba Press and from 1981 to 1999 she was the co-editor (with Barrett Watten) of *Poetics Journal.* She is currently the co-director (with Travis Ortiz) of Atelos, a literary project commissioning and publishing cross-genre work by poets. In the spring of 2007, she was elected a Chancellor of the Academy of American Poets. She teaches in the English Department at the University of California, Berkeley.